The Production of Knowledge

The Production of Knowledge

The Challenge of Social Science Research

William H. Starbuck

OXFORD
UNIVERSITY PRESS

OXFORD
UNIVERSITY PRESS

Great Clarendon Street, Oxford OX2 6DP

Oxford University Press is a department of the University of Oxford.
It furthers the University's objective of excellence in research, scholarship,
and education by publishing worldwide in

Oxford New York

Auckland Cape Town Dar es Salaam Hong Kong Karachi
Kuala Lumpur Madrid Melbourne Mexico City Nairobi
New Delhi Shanghai Taipei Toronto

With offices in

Argentina Austria Brazil Chile Czech Republic France Greece
Guatemala Hungary Italy Japan Poland Portugal Singapore
South Korea Switzerland Thailand Turkey Ukraine Vietnam

Oxford is a registered trade mark of Oxford University Press
in the UK and in certain other countries

Published in the United States
by Oxford University Press Inc., New York

© William H. Starbuck 2006

British Library Cataloguing in Publication Data

Data available

Library of Congress Cataloging in Publication Data

Data available

Typeset by SPI Publisher Services, Pondicherry, India
Printed in Great Britain
on acid-free paper by
Biddles Ltd., King's Lynn,
Norfolk

ISBN 0–19–928853–4   978–0–19–928853–3

1 3 5 7 9 10 8 6 4 2

Contents

List of Figures

List of Tables

1

Creating Better Social Science

During the thirteenth century, professors at the University of Paris decided to find out whether oil would congeal if left outdoors on a cold night. They launched a research project to investigate this question. To them, research meant searching through the works of Aristotle. After much effort, they found that nothing Aristotle had written answered their question, so they declared the question unanswerable.

The essential truth of that anecdote is that the Parisian professors were right: their question was unanswerable within the research tradition to which they conformed. Research findings often tell more about the researchers' tactics than about the phenomena studied, the tactics being shaped by the culture in which research takes place. Because some research tactics are more likely to yield useful results, a culture that endorses such tactics is crucial. Because all research tactics have deficiencies, a culture that endorses the development of better tactics is also crucial.

This book is partly a cry of protest, partly an advocacy for reform, and partly an expression of hope. The protest asserts that many of the research tactics in widespread use are not actually helping humans to understand themselves and their environments. Years pass with negligible gains in usable knowledge; successive studies of a topic appear to explain less and less; the vast majority of published studies present results that are never reproduced. The advocacy argues that alternative research tactics would be more effective. Obviously, if current tactics are ineffective, there is little to be lost from experimenting with alternatives, but there is also reason to believe that some alternatives have demonstrated their value. The hope arises from conviction that social scientists would like to conduct research more effectively, and from awareness that many social scientists are dissatisfied with the current state of affairs. In addition to those who have published appeals for reform, multitudes express disillusionment with the cynicism and opportunism apparent in their fields.

Reform will require widespread support because, with the exception of those disillusioned souls who have given up research without even attempting it, all social scientists are complicit in the failures of social science research. I include myself among the contributors to these failures. Everyone who has used a statistical technique inappropriately has endorsed such misuse, as has everyone who has trumpeted that 'statistical significance' indicates importance. Everyone who has interpreted retrospective research as making predictions has assumed that people or social systems are stable and nonreactive. Everyone who has attacked research on grounds of logic alone has said that human physiology should dominate environmental complexity, because logic is a property of human physiology. Everyone who has submitted an article to a journal has implicitly approved the editorial practices of that journal, and everyone who has submitted to a more prestigious journal in preference to a lower-status, but more appropriate, journal has given social achievement a higher priority than substantive integration.

The book's structure is somewhat unusual: two unusually long autobiographical chapters, 2 and 4, serve as explanatory prefaces to two chapters, 3 and 5, that summarize my arguments. This structure resulted from my interactions with a group of outstanding British researchers, the Fellows of the Advanced Institute of Management Research, who invited me to explain my projected book to them. Since my actual plans for the book were rather vague and I had only a few days to prepare the talk, I decided to tell them why I was dissatisfied with prevalent research tactics and then to ask them if I could come back later and tell them why alternative tactics might be better. After I had drawn up an outline of my objections to prevalent research tactics, I decided that a description of some research experiences would be a logical way to explain why I had become critical or skeptical of prevalent tactics. This explanation took the form of an autobiographical journey through a series of research experiences. I asked my audience for their reactions, and they said they liked the autobiographical approach and they would be willing to listen to my proposals for improvement. Therefore, I created a second autobiographical journey to explain my proposals for change. Later, the first autobiographical journey evolved into Chapter 2 in this book, with

Chapter 3 summarizing my objections to prevalent research tactics. The second autobiographical journey became Chapter 4, and Chapter 5 summarizes my proposals for reform.

I report the autobiographical events with rather little interpretation. As a result, these chapters describe mutually inconsistent experiences and they jump around among themes, somewhat like a detective story that involves different crimes and multiple suspects and the slow discovery of clues. In reporting the two journeys, I have tried to maintain temporal consistency. I often do not tell readers the outcomes of my experiences because these outcomes may have materialized years later. I often do not explain the significance of experiences because I did not understand their significance at the time. It is my assumption that most readers will enjoy weighing my experiences as I was trying to do at the time. I describe my errors and misperceptions, partly to keep myself honest and partly to demonstrate that I am aware that I do not have all the answers.

The two journeys point to more issues than appear in the two summary chapters, mainly because I want to emphasize some issues more than others. Chapter 3 looks at aspects of the theme that researchers do what serves them personally in preference to what promotes the creation of reliable knowledge. Because researchers hold different beliefs about the existence and nature of knowledge and because research practices preserve the uncertainty of what is accepted as known, there is never a closure to research questions and never an end to ambiguity. Because researchers focus on producing journal articles rather than knowledge and because all researchers can claim to have made discoveries, there are no limits to researchers' potential productivity and every researcher can be an unchallenged genius. Because contributions to knowledge echo the properties of human bodies and social systems, nearly all research reveals more about the researchers themselves and their assumptions than about the topics they study. The general effect is that research becomes ritualized pretence rather than a source of genuine contributions to knowledge.

Although researchers have reason to appreciate a social system that allows large numbers of them to appear to be highly productive, the system imposes costs. Hundreds of thousands of talented researchers are producing little or nothing of lasting value. Because the usefulness of their research is so low, their social environment pays little attention to their research and regards them with amused indulgence.

Many researchers lose the idealism that brought them to their occupation originally, as they shift their priorities to social goals such as tenure and promotions. Seeing that their activities are benefiting no one, some researchers come to see themselves as having obligations to no one but themselves, and they engage in egocentric demands.

For social science research to have more value for society at large and to bring greater respect to researchers themselves, researchers must set higher standards for the dependability of findings. Chapter 5 concentrates on research tactics that would improve the relevance and dependability of findings. Although these tactics would certainly not solve all problems, the tactics can yield more robust knowledge that depends less strongly on who did the research. The chapter advocates that researchers should both challenge their own thinking by disrupting their preconceptions and try to demonstrate the validity of their knowledge by observing natural experiments and by displacing situations from equilibria. An ensuing section of the chapter draws attention to statistical methods that emphasize the production of dependable, robust knowledge. Recognizing that knowledge is essentially human and social, the final section urges researchers to strive to create consensus about what we know—the 'facts' we have established and the generality and limitations of these facts.

Acknowledgments

So many people have significantly influenced my thinking that I must rely on the text to acknowledge them. Mikelle Calhoun, Gino Cattani, Roger Dunbar, Alan Meyer, and Danny Miller were kind enough to offer suggestions regarding a draft of this book.

2

A Journey into Disillusionment— Discovering Problems

This chapter describes one side of my intellectual journey, events that exposed problems with research methodology and problems with my conceptualizations of topics. A later chapter will describe a parallel and complementary side of this journey, events that suggested possible solutions to these problems. With benefit of hindsight, I think it is better to describe the range of problems I encountered before attempting to prescribe solutions for some of them. However, a focus on problems gives this chapter a pervasive theme of disappointment.

My account is generally chronological. Although a chronological approach is episodic and somewhat confusing, fragmentation and confusion were intrinsic to my journey and they are characteristics that many readers will recognize in their own experience. Almost all researchers undergo intellectual journeys as they investigate different topics and try different research methods. Of course, each person's journey has distinctive elements, but I am hoping that many social scientists recognize familiar issues as they read my account.

Although I have tried to report accurately, I am unable to make my account entirely factual. Research says that no one remembers events accurately: our brains involuntarily change our memories to make events seem likely and logical, and remembered details are often fictional. I have not kept a diary and have retained precious few old documents, so some dating is conjectural and time has warped what I remember. For that matter, objective facts about many of these events likely never existed, in that other people saw the differently than I.

2.1 The 1950s

While I was in graduate school and for several years thereafter, I believed that rational thought was a tool that one could use to produce understanding. Both my physical and social environments were real, I believed, and I wanted to understand the realities of human and social behavior. I imagined that laws govern human behavior, and these laws, when researchers discovered them, would be as universal and timeless as the laws of physics or chemistry. The paucity of such laws was mainly due, I supposed, to the lack of rigor in psychological and social science methodology. I wanted to help create a true 'behavioral science' based on mathematical models, computer simulation, and systematic experiments.

I had acquired these views in high school, college, and graduate school. Even during high school, I had decided that I wanted to become a scientist, probably a physicist. I then studied science in college, including graduate-level courses in mathematics and electronic engineering, which I found more interesting than physics per se. My science teachers had emphasized the reliability of mathematical formulations and systematic experiments, so it seemed obvious to me that behavioral research had been lacking both in mathematical theories and in systematic experiments.

I developed an interest in computers early in the 1950s. Shortly after I entered college, I had read Wiener's *Cybernetics, or, Control and Communication in the Animal and the Machine* (1948) and Diebold's *Automation: The Advent of the Automatic Factory* (1952), and developed a strong interest in computers. When IBM sent a Harvard alumnus to hire research personnel, I sought a summer job and participated in the engineering of IBM's first large computers—the binary 701 in 1954 and the decimal 705 in 1955.

I decided to earn a doctorate in applied mathematics and then to become a computer designer, probably at IBM. However, largely because I wanted to improve my relationship with my father, I chose first to obtain a master's degree in industrial administration at Carnegie Institute of Technology. My master's studies turned into doctoral ones after Dick Cyert and Jim March hired me to run some experiments (Starbuck 1993a). Computer enthusiast that I was, instead of actually running the experiments myself, I designed an electronic system that ran the experiments automatically and recorded the data. Cyert and March offered to pay my tuition fee as well as a livable stipend if I would become a doctoral student; so I did.

While preparing for the doctoral qualifying examinations, I was awestruck by a chapter about laboratory studies of small group behavior that Kelley and Thibaut (1954) had written for the *Handbook of Social Psychology*. They had masterfully integrated hundreds of experiments, and imposed understanding on confusion. Their chapter was so revolutionary that every social psychologist simply had to read it, and their analysis so impressed me that I chose social psychology as my major field.

During my doctoral studies, I heard Herb Simon advocate the value of mathematical modeling, and I took a course in 'mathematical social science' taught by Alan Newell. Newell and Simon wrote computer programs that modeled human problem-solving, and Cyert and March created simulation programs that imitated the decision processes of managers and companies. I attempted several doctoral dissertations, one of which involved a computer simulation of a large division of the Koppers Company and two of which involved mathematical modeling. I believed computers would allow much greater theoretical complexity than algebra, and I deemed such complexity as not only desirable but also necessary for adequate description of human and social behavior.

* * *

I also heard Herb Simon tell us to use passive verbs. At that time, the American Psychological Association's guidelines for authors forbade the use of first-person and second-person pronouns. This restriction matched widespread norms that said scientists should be objective and should not allow their personal values to influence their research, and hence that scientific writing should convey impersonal detachment. Simon pointed out that this restriction implied that one should use passive verbs because they did not require that one specify who had taken actions. For example, instead of saying 'I gathered data in Cleveland', one should say, 'Data were gathered in Cleveland'. Only a few years later, I began to discover the harmful consequences of such wording.

2.2 The 1960s

Shortly after I began my first academic employment at Purdue University, two of my new colleagues, Ed Ames and Stan Reiter, published an empirical study that I regarded as a curiosity at the time but that strongly influenced my methodological insights more than twenty-five years later. The successive values of a variable over time are called a 'time series'. Ames and Reiter were skeptical of macroeconomists' efforts to develop understanding of relations among economic variables by looking at correlations between time series of these variables. Social scientists often calculate correlations between time series—for example, the correlation between the number of operating steel mills and gross national product (GNP). However, most time series pose challenges for reliable induction because they autocorrelate rather strongly; that is, later values correlate with earlier values. High autocorrelations produce high correlations between series that have nothing to do with causal links between those series. As a result, social scientists find it easy to discover high correlations between series even when series have no direct causal relations (Peach and Webb 1983).

Ames and Reiter (1961) demonstrated the practical implications of autocorrelations by studying actual socioeconomic series. They plucked 100 series at random from *Historical Statistics for the United States*. Each series spanned the twenty-five years from 1929 to 1953. For a one-year lag, five-sixths of the series had autocorrelations above 0.8 and the mean autocorrelation was 0.837. Even after Ames and Reiter removed linear trends from the series, the mean autocorrelation was 0.675 for a one-year lag. Autocorrelations generally decline as longer lags separate the correlated values. Ames and Reiter found mean autocorrelations of 0.599 for a three-year lag and 0.453 for a five-year lag. Even a correlation of 0.45 indicates rather strong similarity.

Next, Ames and Reiter correlated randomly selected series. They found an average (absolute value) correlation of 0.571 between random pairs of series. For 46 percent of these random pairs, there existed a time lag of zero to five years that made the two series correlate at least 0.7.

Finally, Ames and Reiter simulated the widespread practice of searching for highly correlated pairs of series. They picked a target series at random, and then compared this series with other series that they also picked randomly. On average, they needed only three trials to draw a second series that correlated highly enough with the target series that it appeared to 'explain' at least half the variance in the target series. Even after they corrected all series for linear trends, they needed only five trials on average to draw a series that seemed to 'explain' at least half the variance in a target series.

Thus, a lesson about the unreliability of inferences from empirical data christened my career, although I did not fully appreciate the implications of Ames and Reiter's study at that time.

* * *

My own research during the 1960s involved mathematical models, laboratory experiments, and computer simulation. My experiments focused on choices made by individual people (now called behavioral decision theory), negotiations between two people, and teams of students managing hypothetical companies that competed against each other in computer-based markets. In promoting experimentation, I collaborated with Vernon Smith, who was pioneering experimental approaches to economic behavior, for which he later received the Nobel Prize in Economic Sciences. Vernon invited me to join him in seeking a large research grant, and he and I jointly obtained funding, designed, and built a laboratory for experimental research (Fromkin 1969). I conceived the laboratory's unique electronic system that ran experiments automatically, a larger-scale descendant of the device I had built while a doctoral student.

My enthusiasm for experiments waned in the mid-1960s after I attended a workshop about experimental studies of economic behavior. Although the organizers of this conference intended it to reinforce interest in experimental economics, it had quite the opposite effect on me. The experiments we discussed and ran showed me the supreme importance of having 'subjects' who sincerely want to help an experimenter. Willing subjects try to obey researchers' instructions, but subjects who want to undermine an experiment can easily do so.

The organizers of the workshop inadvertently facilitated a telling example of experimentation gone wrong. During the first session, the organizers told us that they had promised on our behalf that we attendees would all be subjects in an experiment run by one of the attendees. Several attendees bridled immediately at the idea they were being required to participate involuntarily. The experimenter then divided us into groups of three competitors, asking each person to pretend to be making bids in a three-person market. The experimenter next handed us written instructions and told us to read them. When people attempted to ask questions about the instructions, the experimenter gave terse responses or dismissed the questions as trivial. I recall someone, possibly myself, pointing out that the instructions said 'There will be no collusion detectable by the experimenter', and asking 'Does this mean that you do not want us to collude?' The experimenter replied, 'Just follow the instructions on the paper.'

As soon as we had an opportunity, my two 'competitors' and I met privately to discuss how we could collude in a way that the experimenter would be unable to detect. We decided that the bid prices in our market would rise monotonically, and that the exact increases and the identities of the winning bidders would be determined by random events such as the number of words spoken by the experimenter when asking us to submit bids. None of us aspired to perform well according to the experiment's performance criteria, that is, to make imaginary profits in our imaginary industry. All of us enjoyed proving that we could outwit the experimenter. We later discovered that several other groups of three competitors had also met privately to discuss how they could collude, and each group had invented an artificial behavior pattern that they expected to go against the experimenter's expectations.

Of course, this was an extreme situation created by a rather smug and inflexible experimenter who showed indifference toward subjects who were being compelled to participate. Most subjects try to follow an experimenter's instructions insofar as they can understand what the experimenter wants. However, as I saw it, this observation highlighted the most vital point—experimenters can control their subjects' behaviors to high degrees. If experimenters attract willing subjects and give them complete and precise instructions, nearly all subjects make every effort to carry out these instructions. Insofar as experimenters give ambiguous instructions, the subjects act as they please and different subjects are likely to act differently. For example, if an experimenter tells subjects 'Try to earn as much money as you can', the subjects will act as if money is their primary goal, and nearly all will do this even if the amounts of money seem trivial to them. Of course, experimenters can take steps to assure that their subjects understand their instructions and to motivate them to follow the instructions carefully. For instance, experimenters can offer larger monetary payments, they can make actual cash payments immediately, or they may even be able to induce sympathy.

Over a few years, I also concluded that normal experiments are not useful. Because people are so flexible and versatile, it is rarely worthwhile to show that they are capable of certain behaviors. One has to show that certain behaviors occur under realistic conditions—realistic incentives, realistic training, realistic amounts of experience, and realistic processes for selecting participants and assigning tasks to them. Yet, an experimenter cannot approximate in a laboratory the rewards and socialization experiences that occur in real-life organizations. Outside the laboratory, people come to know each other over months and years; they may participate in months or years of training, and their rewards may involve significant wage changes, promotions, social statuses that persist for years, and long-term consequences from short-term actions.

Thus, I began to view laboratory experiments as exercises in the writing of instructions and the motivation of subjects, who would then perform tasks having little significance outside the laboratory. I could elicit behaviors I wanted by writing instructions that were clear and complete enough, and by making sure that the subjects understood the instructions and wanted to follow them. But was this a useful goal? To demonstrate that I could write instructions and persuade subjects to follow them? Certainly, the results from my experiments strongly reflected my own goals and my own beliefs about what behaviors I wanted to observe, even when I had had little insight about these beforehand. Thus, my experiments were revealing a lot about my own beliefs and very little about my subjects' properties other than their obedience. Was this not a silly game to be playing? Indeed, in the end, I never submitted most of my laboratory studies to journals because the studies seemed worthless to me and I could not motivate myself to write articles based on such a flawed methodology. This was, of course, very bad behavior on my part because it meant that I had few publications to show for many months of work and I had no publications to report to the National Science Foundation, which had funded my experiments.

*   *   *

As I grew more skeptical of laboratory experimentation, I came to see it as surprisingly similar to computer simulation. Simulators try to write programs that correctly express their assumptions; computers' actions demonstrate implications of the researchers' programs; and if the programs accurately represent the researchers' assumptions, the computers' actions demonstrate logical implications of the researchers' assumptions (Starbuck and Dutton 1971; Starbuck 1983a). Thus, computer simulation is supposed to aid deduction. Computer simulation differs from laboratory experimentation in that simulators can rely on computers to follow instructions exactly, whereas experimenters have to motivate their subjects to follow instructions. Of course, computers can do only what they have been instructed to do, whereas subjects in experiments are capable of inventing instructions for themselves.

In an effort to promote the wider use of simulation and to make its use more rigorous, John Dutton and I coedited an anthology about computer simulations of human behavior (Dutton and Starbuck 1971a). We also spent six years, on and off, trying to understand and simulate a production scheduler named Charlie. One series of experiments gave us a lot of insight into what one needs to understand human behavior and to create theories about it. One winter, we focused on an estimating task that Charlie performed many times each day, and we ran 577 experiments on this tiny segment of his behavior. The experiments showed us how he thought, how we could model his thoughts, and why a realistic simulation of his thought-processes was actually less informative than an abstract algebraic model. These experiments worked well partly because we devoted an incredible amount of effort to one tiny activity and partly because Charlie himself helped us to design revealing experiments (Dutton and Starbuck 1967, 1971b).

Mathematical analysis can aid deduction in much the same way as computer simulation. When creating a mathematical model, one states assumptions and then uses algebra to extract implications of these assumptions. One can try out different assumptions until the model exhibits properties one desires, and in some cases, one can characterize sets of assumptions that lead to specific properties. When algebraic analyses are feasible, they are more useful than computer simulations because algebraic expressions relate assumptions and implications more clearly and more generally. Therefore, one should do computer simulation mainly when one does not know how to model a theory mathematically.

Algebraic analyses are often infeasible. In particular, mathematical formulations are difficult to manipulate unless one limits the mathematics to linear functions; linear formulations remain solvable even if they include many, many equations. Nearly all nonlinear functions pose insurmountable analytic challenges, especially when the formulations involve several equations. The nonlinear functions include ones that change in different directions for different values of the variables and ones that involve abrupt branching—if A, then B; if not A, then C. Computer simulation allows researchers to develop flawlessly the logical implications of nonlinear assumptions, and computers impose very weak restrictions on the complexity of models. In principle, simulation can disclose the consequences of a multitude of nonlinear, discontinuous, interacting assumptions.

Simulation lays traps for the unwary. A multitude of nonlinear, discontinuous, interacting assumptions has the potential to generate outputs that appear mysterious, even magical. Because simulations carry out processes step-by-step, researchers have to specify processes step-by-step even when they lack adequate information about them. Large, complex simulation models are virtually impossible to validate in detail because needed information does not exist. One dare not infer the processes that generated outcomes from the outcomes alone because many different processes might generate very similar outputs. Computers generate outputs without explaining their reasoning. Researchers can add instructions to their programs that record calculation sequences but simulation programs typically incorporate so many microscopic steps that the explanations themselves pose serious data-analysis challenges. As a result, researchers are likely to be unable to understand the causes of simulated behaviors.

In this fashion, simulation confronts Bonini's paradox. As I phrase it, Bonini's paradox is 'As a model grows more realistic it also becomes just as difficult to understand as the real-world processes it represents.' A researcher builds a model to gain or demonstrate understanding of a causal process, and the researcher states this model as a computer simulation with complex assumptions that the researcher believes to be realistic. The resulting simulation generates outputs that may resemble those observed in the modeled situation. However, the model itself is very complex, and the interdependences between subroutines are obscure, so the model is just as difficult to understand as the causal process being modeled.

I call this phenomenon Bonini's paradox because I first encountered it in the context of Chuck Bonini's doctoral dissertation. Bonini and I were doctoral students together and we both attempted to create computer simulations of business firms. Chuck was much more successful than I was, for he completed a simulation model and a prize-winning dissertation, whereas I abandoned my effort to model a firm. His model represented a hypothetical firm's detailed decision-making as it decided how much to produce, what prices to charge, and so forth. In a short time, he could generate many years of decision-making, and he could vary elements of both the decision processes and the environment of the firm. Nevertheless, in his dissertation, Bonini (1963: 136) wrote: 'We cannot explain completely the reasons why the firm behaves in a specific fashion. Our model of the firm is highly complex, and it is not possible to trace out the behavior pattern throughout the firm.... Therefore, we cannot pinpoint the explicit causal mechanism in the model.'

It did occur to me that even though complex simulations are very difficult to understand, even very complex simulations are probably much simpler than people are.

*   *   *

In 1966, my efforts to analyze the results of an experiment showed me how deceptive rationality could be as a tool for understanding my world. I was trying to write a paper about the behaviors of teams that had played a business game. I had hired an assistant to run the game and to submit the data for statistical analyses by the university's computer. The result was a pile of computer output about 8 inches thick. However, my efforts to understand the results were going nowhere because the outputs from the statistical analyses differed so greatly from the hypotheses I had held when designing the study. I tried introducing various correction factors but they did not help at all. Therefore, I decided to figure out inductively what the data were telling me. I constructed diagrams that represented high correlations by thick lines and low correlations by thin lines, and then I began to play the game of 'why X correlates with Y but not with Z'. After a couple of weeks, I had constructed a complete and logically integrated explanation for the relations among variables.

Nevertheless, the dramatic differences between my expectations and the actual results nagged at me. Although my induced theory was logical, it was quite at odds with the one I had held when designing the study. I had not had first-hand involvement with the raw data or the calculations because my research assistant had turned the data into statistics. I decided to trace back through all of the statistical analyses;

perhaps close inspection of the data and the analysis process might help me to comprehend the differences between my initial expectations and the findings. To my surprise, I discovered that very early in the analytic process, my assistant had made a small data-entry error that had had great effects. The experiment involved four treatments, so some statistical analyses required adding correction factors that would make the treatments more comparable. When correcting for one of the four treatments, my assistant had omitted two minus signs and so he had inadvertently added instead of subtracted. Instead of becoming comparable with the other three treatments, that treatment had become an extreme outlier, but the subsequent analyses assumed no important differences between treatments. Hence, I had just spent weeks trying to make sense of statistics that contained large systematic errors and the correlations on which I had constructed a theory were utter nonsense. In effect, I had constructed a logically satisfying theory based on random noise. And I had been quite successful!

* * *

One of my early laboratory studies demonstrated that an average statistic might describe very few of the instances included in the average, possibly none of them. Frank Bass and I asked 785 people how much they would be willing to spend to obtain accurate information about the potential market for a new product, and the median answer was exactly equal to the theoretical optimum amount (Starbuck and Bass 1967). However, few people gave answers close to this median; the fraction of people who said they would spend near-optimum amounts for information ranged from 1 to 17 percent.

I began noticing other problems with averages. For instance, a correlation across a population may occur in none of the subpopulations. For example, computing data aggregated across states, Robinson (1950) found a correlation of 0.619 between the percentage of a state's population that was foreign-born and the percentage that could read American English. This correlation might lead someone to infer that foreign-born residents were more likely to be literate in English than were native-born residents. However, the positive state-level correlation occurred because foreign-born people were more likely to reside in states where many residents were literate in English. The correlation computed from data about individuals was negative, -0.118.

* * *

Around 1966 or 1967, I read a theorem about point null hypotheses. (I do not remember what document I actually read. Berkson expressed the basic idea in 1938, but I am sure I did not read his article. Several books and articles about Bayesian statistics appeared between 1959 and 1965, including Schlaifer (1959), Nunnally (1960), Edwards, Lindman, and Savage (1963), and an unpublished text written in 1965 by Pratt, Raiffa, and Schlaifer (1995).)

In school, we learn to construct mathematical proofs by contradiction, in which we demonstrate that a hypothesis cannot possibly be true. For example, we might assume that there exists a largest prime number such that no prime number can exceed this largest one. In proof by contradiction, we might then create a new prime number that is larger than the hypothesized largest one, thus showing that the hypothesis must be false. Null hypothesis significance tests imitate proof by contradiction, but they rely on probabilistic reasoning whereas proof by contradiction relies on conclusive logic. That is, null hypothesis significance tests seek to show that null hypotheses have very small probabilities of being true.

A point null hypothesis is one that defines an infinitesimal point on a continuum. The hypothesis that two sample means are exactly equal is a point hypothesis. Other examples include these null hypotheses:

$$\text{correlation} = 0$$
$$\text{frequency} = 0$$
$$\text{rate} = 0$$
$$\text{regression coefficient} = 0$$
$$\text{variance 1} = \text{variance 2}$$

All 'two-tailed tests' concerning continuous variables use point null hypotheses because they say that one statistic must equal another one exactly.

The theorem I read explained that the probability of rejecting a point null hypothesis rises closer and closer to 1 as the sample size grows toward infinity. Someone who gathers a large enough sample can be very nearly certain of rejecting a point null hypothesis. This theorem follows directly from the fact that a point null hypothesis defines an infinitesimally small point. Any sample statistic one computes from data defines a small range of possible values—a confidence interval. For the null hypothesis to appear possible, the infinitesimal point corresponding to the null hypothesis must lie inside the confidence interval around the computed sample statistic. As the sample size increases, the confidence interval shrinks and becomes less likely to encompass the point corresponding to the null hypothesis. As the sample size goes to infinity, the confidence interval becomes infinitely small and exceedingly unlikely to encompass the infinitesimally small point corresponding to the null hypothesis. There will always remain some tiny likelihood that the point corresponding to the null hypothesis may fall into the confidence interval, but this likelihood decreases as the confidence interval shrinks.

A concrete example may clarify what happens. Suppose that two variables have no relation whatever to each other and the null hypothesis states that the correlation between them equals zero. If the test is to say that the data are consistent with this null hypothesis, the confidence interval around the calculated estimate of the correlation has to encompass the infinitesimal point at zero. However, the numbers used to calculate this estimated correlation are approximate because the method used to measure variables entails some error. This error might only be round-off error because the recorded measurements have, say, four significant digits, or the error might come from imperfect translation of theoretical constructs into measurements, or the error might come from mistakes by the people who provide the data. Even though the correlated variables have no relationship to each other, the errors in measurements mean that the calculated estimate of the correlation is very, very unlikely to be exactly zero, although it may differ from zero by only a tiny amount. As the sample size grows larger and larger, the confidence interval around this calculated estimate shrinks and shrinks, creating the appearance of increasing precision, increasing confidence that the true correlation is almost exactly the calculated estimate. Eventually, with a large enough sample, the statistical analysis will affirm that the observed correlation falls between, say, 0.00000004 and 0.00000005, thus rejecting the null hypothesis that the correlation is zero.

Thus, if data do not already reject a point hypothesis, a researcher can make rejection more likely by making additional observations and reducing the size of the confidence interval. Passing a 'hypothesis test' against such a point null hypothesis tells little about the alternative hypothesis but much about the researcher's perseverance and effort.

This theorem made me aware for the first time that social scientists were misusing statistical significance tests when they acted as if statistical significance indicates the importance of studied phenomena. The importance of phenomena should not depend on how much work a researcher is willing to do. In a way, statistical significance tests are statements about researchers' willingness to invest effort as much as they are statements about the phenomena studied.

Of course, it was also easy to see why social scientists were using significance tests inappropriately. Statistics courses taught one how to perform significance tests and they offered no alternatives to them. Statistical education focused on formulations that statisticians developed early in the twentieth century. In the absence of electronic computers, statisticians needed to concentrate on functions that they could manipulate algebraically, and they needed an approach to analysis that would allow many different researchers to use the same, generic numerical tables. Point null hypotheses made algebra much simpler, and hypotheses about 'no difference' appeared to have applicability to many research situations. One very unfortunate consequence was widespread use of 'tests' that were easy to pass (Loftus 1996).

Tests of point null hypotheses also made me aware of the degree to which research methodologies rest on consensus rather than their effectiveness. Statistical education teaches a specific approach to analyzing data, and nearly all statistics students are happy if they can just understand this approach, so they accept it without challenging its validity. As a result, there is almost no questioning of the premises behind statistical education and no discussion of alternative approaches. I began to think of statistical tests as arcane rituals that demonstrate membership in an esoteric subculture. Since researchers who study very different topics have all studied these rituals, they can all participate in discussions at seminars even if they do not understand or care about the substance of presented research. Indeed, seminars often wander off into statistical discussions that have no relevance to the importance of the studied topic or the importance of the research findings.

* * *

After I moved to Cornell University in 1967, I discovered the ambiguity surrounding human judgments about research findings when I became the editor of *Administrative Science Quarterly* (*ASQ*) in 1968. My predecessor passed on a thigh-high stack of manuscripts that had been awaiting review; he said he had sent no manuscripts out for review for several months because he thought I would like to have a low backlog of accepted articles. Embarrassed that so many authors had been waiting so long for feedback, I weeded out the obviously inappropriate topics and then sent manuscripts to hundreds of reviewers. At that time, *ASQ* was seeking to encompass all aspects of management, so the manuscripts and reviewers were quite diverse. After two or three months, I had received well over 500 pairs of reviews. What struck me most vividly about these reviews were their inconsistency and their blatant biases: A surprisingly small fraction of the reviewers agreed with each other. Counting an 'accept' as 1, a 'revise' as 0, and a 'reject' as -1, I calculated the correlation between reviewers. It was 0.12. Given the large sample size, this correlation was statistically significant but it was practically insignificant. It was so low that knowing what one reviewer had said about a manuscript should tell me almost nothing about what a second reviewer had said or would say. More generally, the reviewers exhibited almost no agreement about what constitutes good research, what findings are credible, what topics are interesting, or what methodology is appropriate. Reviewers from, say, economics wanted authors to base arguments on economic reasoning and to use methodology characteristic of economics, and likewise, sociological reviewers wanted authors to base arguments on sociological reasoning and to use methodology characteristic of sociology. I saw much more than before that research quality is a political judgment, and I began to wonder if cultural differences among social sciences block the development of mutually accepted knowledge.

About 25 percent of the reviews recommended 'accept', about 25 percent recommended 'revise', and about 50 percent recommended 'reject'. If any two reviews are utterly independent, the probability of a manuscript receiving two 'accepts' should be about 25% * 25% = 6 percent and the probability of a manuscript receiving two 'rejects' should be about 50% * 50% = 25 percent. The remaining 69 percent should receive mixed reviews. These frequencies are close to the ones I experienced as *ASQ*'s editor. I responded by accepting the 6 percent that received two 'accepts', rejecting the 25 percent that received two 'rejects', and soliciting revisions from the 69 percent that received mixed reviews. Only about half of the authors whom I invited to revise actually submitted revised manuscripts that differed noticeably from their earlier manuscripts; the other half either submitted very superficial revisions or took their manuscripts elsewhere. Thus, authors' motivation and belief in their work were strongly influencing whether their manuscripts made it into print. Some authors were responding to negative feedback by withdrawing or refusing to comply, whereas other authors were responding by demonstrating persistence and some degree of compliance. Although noisy and inconsistent environments pose challenges, ambiguity was creating opportunities for authors to engineer their personal career success through persistence, adaptation, symbolic behavior, and intelligent marketing.

*   *   *

The late 1960s also introduced me to research that looked suspicious. The first jarring case involved a friend during graduate school. His prize-winning dissertation described a computer simulation of the thought-processes of a man who managed investments, and no one had previously simulated such complex decision-making and obtained such close correspondence between the behavior of the simulation model and the behavior of the person. In 1967, I began to write a book about decision-making and planned to devote the third chapter to my friend's outstanding dissertation research. To explain it well, I needed to understand it thoroughly, so I pored over it for ten weeks, digesting every word and trying to reproduce every detail. I even traveled across the USA and interviewed the investment manager who had been modeled.

The more thoroughly I read the dissertation, the less sense it made and the more contradictions surfaced. The theory would not generate the sequences of analyses that the dissertation attributed to it. Neither the theory nor the analytic sequences would produce the decisions that the dissertation attributed to them. The decision-maker said he had eagerly read the dissertation but had seen little resemblance between the theory and his thought-processes, so he was surprised that the theory produced decisions so similar to his. I had to conclude that this famous study should probably be infamous. I was so disillusioned and disgusted that I threw away my book manuscript and refunded the publisher's advance (Starbuck and Dutton 1971).

A second case also involved a dissertation. Chick Perrow sent me a note expressing concerns about the credibility of a manuscript that *ASQ* had recently accepted for publication. In his reaction to the original version, Chick had asked for interview evidence. Two months after receiving this feedback, the author submitted a revision that

Table 2.1 Newly submitted data

	Result A	Result B	Result C
Condition 1	0 %	5 %	95 %
Condition 2	25 %	50 %	25 %
Condition 3	95 %	5 %	0 %

included data from 700 interviews conducted in fifty companies. However, the interview evidence seemed strangely tidy. The statistics looked very much like Table 2.1.

Suspicious, Chick had traveled to another state, gone to the university library, and examined the dissertation from which the manuscript derived. His note to me reported that he had found no interviews in the dissertation. Evidently, the author had conducted the interviews after receiving the reviewers' reactions to the original version, but no one could conduct 700 interviews in fifty companies in two months.

I told the author that *ASQ* would not publish his manuscript. He demanded a hearing. I recruited a review panel of sociologists and asked the author to bring all of his data to a meeting. He arrived bearing only a large deck of punched cards. We asked to see his notes from the interviews he had conducted three to four months earlier. He said that he had destroyed his notes after he recorded the data on punched cards. We examined the punched cards. The large deck turned out to be many copies of the same fifty cards, one card for each company. The only information on the cards was the information tabulated in his article.

The review panel upheld the decision not to publish. The panel also wrote to the American Sociological Association, suggesting that they publish a warning about an article that the *American Sociological Review* had published by this author and based on these data. The Association replied that their lawyer had advised them not to publish such a warning 'because that would be picking out one article as an exception'.

2.3 The 1970s

In 1970, I began a year as a Fulbright Fellow at London Business School, a year that brought several intellectual surprises.

In the process of writing about relations between organizations and their environments (Starbuck 1976), I gradually came to see that organizations are not clearly distinct from their environments, that boundaries between organization and environment are not at all discrete. In fact, boundaries between organization and environment are, to no small degree, inventions of the observers. Although some activities might be clearly internal to a specific organization and some activities might be clearly external to that organization, many activities involve interactions in which both organization and environment participate. As a result, there is no clear point at which internal ceases and external begins.

Then I began to think about how to measure the degree to which someone or some activity occupies a position near the center of an organization versus out at its periphery. I explored this idea by calculating variables that described people in the company that employed Charlie, the production scheduler that Dutton and I had tried to simulate. Several possible measures were mutually at odds. For example, according to some measures, the company's president would be central to the company, but according to other measures, the president would be far out on the periphery. Not only can the boundaries between organization and environment depend on what activities an observer considers but also the boundaries can vary from time to time. As well, each organization interacts with several different kinds of environments—legal, financial, social, transportation, technological, and so on.

One result was that I began to see organizations less and less as distinct social systems, and more and more as arbitrary categories created by observers or social conventions. The phenomena that I had previously regarded as objectively real were vaporizing into mental and social constructions.

* * *

Derek Pugh headed a research group at London Business School that met weekly to discuss their progress. They called their research the Aston Studies because they (and others) had begun making such studies at the University of Aston. Their research activity involved creating and filling out questionnaires to describe organizations, and then making statistical analyses of these data. They mainly used significance tests, factor analysis, and regression. Their methods resembled those of other leading researchers at that time, and indeed, much the same as the dominant methods of today. As the editor of

ASQ, I had been very happy to publish their articles as exemplars of methodology that was, at that time, rather avant-garde.

As I listened to them discuss their work, I began to think that this methodology was nearly blind to the most important social phenomena. The world they perceived was entirely static. Everything was in equilibrium; changes did not occur; no one was challenging authority or asking for different rules. Of course, many social scientists focus exclusively on equilibria, either because equilibria support simpler theories or because cross-section studies provide no basis for discussing change.

However, several influences made me a skeptical audience for discussions that disregarded the possibility of change. One of the dissertations I had never completed had dealt with people's aspirations, especially their desires to accomplish some goals as quickly as possible (Starbuck 1964). I had also been writing about organizational growth, development, and metamorphosis, which are most definitely not equilibria (Starbuck 1965, 1968). Dutton and I had studied another developmental process, the history of computer simulation (Starbuck and Dutton 1971). As well, I was thinking and proposing that evolution might afford an effective framework for viewing organizations' interactions with their environments (Starbuck 1976).

My first reaction was to urge the Aston researchers to investigate change, but I also started to think more generally about the kinds of data that social scientists use and the worlds they perceive. Disregard of change is only part of the problem. Social scientists also focus exclusively on spontaneous phenomena—those that occur without stimulus or intervention by researchers. Spontaneous phenomena can be interesting but they tend to be uninteresting because they dominated statistically by familiar events—nearly every adult has brown eyes, nearly all rock formations fall into a few prevalent categories and they do not contain diamonds or precious metals, patients tell their psychiatrists what they want the psychiatrists to hear. Spontaneous data generally describe aspects of systems that are in or near equilibria, and these aspects may be stable either because they are not important enough for someone to contest them or because they satisfy constraints so important that no one dares to challenge them. As well, spontaneous data generally reflect political interests. I remembered my uncompleted effort to construct a computer simulation of a division of the Koppers Company. I had begun gathering data in the division's headquarters; but some data were missing, so I looked at the data that one of the factories had retained. I then discovered that the data at the factory differed significantly from the data that the factory had sent to headquarters, which portrayed the factory as being more profitable. When I investigated the data at two other factories, I found similar differences. I abandoned the project because I was unable to decide whether I should be modeling the company that existed in the factories or the company that existed at headquarters. At that time, the idea that two realities might exist, neither of which was truly real, was beyond my imagination.

Howard Aldrich (1972) had also been looking at the Aston studies, but from a perspective very different from mine. He believed that a new statistical method—path analysis—showed that the Aston group had drawn incorrect inferences. Aldrich said that path analysis was superior to regression because it forced researchers to articulate one-way causal relations that included all of the important influences on the endogenous variables the theory was supposed to explain. These strong requirements would enable researchers to draw stronger inferences, he said. I saw a parallel. I had seen that simulation required researchers to fulfill strong requirements in order to make their programs run—to provide very detailed information about causal processes—and one result had been that researchers concocted all sorts of assumptions to make their programs run.

To respond to Aldrich's critique, Pugh recruited Gordon Hilton (1972), who advanced arguments that impressed me. Hilton showed that the Aston data were consistent with three alternative theories: the one advanced by the Aston group, the one advanced by Aldrich, and a theory that combined elements of both of the other theories. Hilton (1972: 53) then remarked: 'The causal inference technique would hopefully reject nonsense networks, but so would a priori thinking. Data will always be consistent with several different theories. The choice among these alternatives must be made on other grounds.' He also pointed out that causal inference techniques do not actually identify directions of causation: 'The data determine only the magnitude of the relationship, not the direction of the relationship; all so-called conclusions about the direction of a relationship are not conclusions but assumptions' (Hilton 1972: 54).

* * *

In 1971, I moved to Berlin, where I was startled by some German professors' perception of American research as being mindless empiricism. One of them likened American social scientists to hamsters running on exercise wheels—they run and run and run frantically, but go nowhere. Not initially, of course, but eventually I came to see that much empirical research imitates prior research and adds nothing of value, except more lines on résumés. A few years later, after I had come to admire the insights of several European scholars, I returned to the USA and encountered the other side of this coin—Americans who were exceedingly proud of the superiority of American empiricism and disdainful of the less empirical European social science. Indeed, as I migrated to other countries over the ensuing years, I discovered that every country in which I lived cherished beliefs about the superiority of its intelligentsia, educational institutions, and intellectual traditions.

* * *

While in Berlin, I read Wold's graphic introduction (1965) to time series analysis. Wold used computer simulations to demonstrate how far series diverge from their expected values when new values of a series depend upon its prior values. Real-world examples might include a series of monthly national employment figures, a series of daily closing prices for Wal-Mart stock, or a series of daily average temperatures in Lake Erie. Wold assumed three very simple models of how such series might occur, generated series from these models, and then tried to infer which of the three models had generated the series. When he looked at a single instance of a series having 100 consecutive observations, inference was hopeless. He could make fairly accurate estimates of central tendencies when he made 200 replications with 100 events in each series—20,000 observations—but no social process remains stable while generating so many events.

Inference is unreliable because a series that depends causally on its own past values amplifies and perpetuates random disturbances. Such a process does not forget random disturbances instantly; it reacts to random disturbances when generating future outcomes. Each replication of such a process can generate very different series that diverge erratically from their expected values. An implication is that observed series provide weak evidence about the processes that generated them. A single series or a few replications are very likely to suggest incorrect inferences (Pant and Starbuck 1990).

Wold used very simple one-variable equations to generate series. Such simple processes are uncommon in socioeconomic analyses. To imitate the kinds of statistical inferences that social scientists usually try to draw from longitudinal data, I extended Wold's work by generating autocorrelated series with the properties that Ames and Reiter had observed: Each series included a linear time trend and was second-order autocorrelated with an autocorrelation coefficient above 0.6. Each series included twenty-five events, a length typical of published studies. Each analysis involved three series: series Y depended causally on series X; but series W was causally independent of both X and Y.

Using accepted procedures for time series, I then estimated the coefficients of an equation that erroneously hypothesized that Y depended upon both X and W. The coefficient estimates nearly always showed a statistically significant correlation between Y and W—a reminder of the often ignored injunction that correlation does not equal causation. The modal coefficient estimates were reasonably accurate; most of the errors fell between 10 percent and 50 percent. However, estimates of coefficients that were close to zero had huge percentage errors.

Because Wold had shown that replications led to better estimates of central tendencies, I expected replications to allow better estimates of the coefficients. I wanted to find out how many replications one might need to distinguish causal dependence from independence with a misspecified model. To my surprise, although the result seemed obvious in retrospect, replications proved harmful almost as often as helpful: Nearly 40 percent of the time, the very first series analyzed produced more-accurate-than-average coefficient estimates, and so replications made the average errors worse. Thus, replication might foster confidence in coefficient estimates while actually decreasing the average accuracy of these estimates.

*   *   *

I was interested in time series because I wanted to analyze statistical data on the revolutions in German universities that had occurred a few years earlier. Despite my growing skepticism about the trustworthiness of rational thought, I had continued to publish articles that incorporated mathematical reasoning, and I had written an article that characterized mathematically the conditions needed for a social system to undergo a rapid dramatic revolution (Starbuck 1973). The mathematics suggests that it is not meaningful to try to explain why such revolutions begin; one can specify the time when a revolution began but not why it began at that time.

I wanted to see whether I could develop a mathematical description of a system that had actually had a revolution. Although the occurrence of a revolution implied that the German universities would have had the mathematically necessary properties, I was curious what character these properties might have had in a real-life revolution. I went into the library of the Free University and began to record numbers, and what I found was that the revolution had changed the data that people had collected. The variables that people had observed before the revolution were ones relating to the system that existed before the revolution; they did not include the variables that became relevant after the revolution. And symmetrically, the variables that people observed after the revolution were ones relating to the system that existed after the revolution; people had stopped observing the variables that had been relevant before the revolution. Indeed, after the revolution, the university continued to gather very few of the data it had compiled before the revolution; and conversely, before the revolution, the university had gathered very few of the data it was gathering after the revolution. This experience reinforced my wariness about spontaneous data by demonstrating even more clearly that many data have political coloration—political in the sense that they represent the interests of controlling elites.

* * *

My article about the mathematics of revolutionary social systems induced me to stop writing mathematical articles. I thought my analysis was very interesting, but it appeared to me that very few other people were interested in reading articles containing advanced mathematics. I decided not to waste my life writing articles that few read.

My desire to write more widely read articles made me an apt consumer of ideas about writing style, and I read an article about overuse of the verb 'to be'. This article pointed out that 'to be' often makes writing less interesting by portraying situations as static, in equilibrium, balanced. It struck me that 'to be' also encourages social scientists to create static frames of reference, to view social worlds as stable, and thus to overlook dynamic events.

* * *

A colleague, Bo Hedberg, announced that he had received a research grant from the Swedish government to study stagnating industries.

He said that he wanted to find out why some industries stagnate and drive firms out of business and put people out of work.

Possibly because my background and orientation are social-psychological, I was inclined to place the responsibility upon the firms rather than their environments. I said something tactful like: 'Bo, your thinking is all screwed up! The interesting question is not why do some industries stagnate. Technologies are always developing; populations are always migrating, prices are always shifting—it's inevitable that things will change, and some changes will render some industries obsolete. The relevant question is: Why do intelligent people who are running a firm choose to remain in a stagnating industry even though they recognize that it's stagnating? Why don't firms move into more promising industries when their current ones start to stagnate?'

With similar tact, Hedberg responded, approximately: 'You're spinning an academic fantasy. A firm that knows how to make and sell something can't just pick up their product line and their engineers and plunge into another industry. Their specialized skills and business connections make them captives of their environment. The firms in an industry have to evolve together. It's a societal problem to create incentives that keep industries vital, that keep them evolving in line with social needs and economic and technological opportunities.'

Obviously, we disagreed greatly: I was saying industrial stagnation posed problems for the managers of individual firms, whereas Hedberg was saying industrial stagnation posed problems for government policymakers. We decided to resolve our disagreement by investigating these issues together. When Hedberg and I moved to Milwaukee, Paul Nystrom joined us, and the three of us began a collaboration that continued for ten years.

Among the results of our collaboration were case studies of organizations facing crises. We chose to make case studies because we thought initially that we were looking for unusual events and we wanted to see how these unusual events developed over time. We thought that nearly all organizations and industries go along fairly successfully most of the time, but that once in a while, a disease, much like a virus or a bacterium, infects an organization or an industry and makes it ill. When the disease is very serious, the afflicted organization or industry suddenly faces a crisis that it cannot survive and it goes out of business. We began searching for organizations that were facing very serious crises so that we could investigate what caused them to get into so much trouble and what actions they took while they were in it.

Of course, our argument meant that we did not look specifically for organizations that got into trouble because of changes in their environments. We did not exclude such cases, but environmental change was not a criterion for choosing cases to study. We just looked for signs of serious trouble, and we looked for diverse kinds of organizations, industries, or signs of trouble.

What we found was not what we had expected when we started. For example, we were inundated with examples! Crises appeared wherever we looked. They infested our newspapers and magazines; our colleagues pointed them out to us; skeptics in our audiences brought us examples. It gradually dawned on us that we were seeing normality, that failures and serious threats of them are commonplace. Almost every organization confronts a serious crisis at some time, and some survive repeated crises.

Our initial disagreement stimulated us to consider alternative interpretations of events, and several of our key inferences came to us only after years of debate and over the initial resistance of one or more of us. One inference we had much trouble drawing was that crises are prevalent because the actions organizations take to ensure success also cause crises (Miller 1990). Successful organizations try to continue succeeding by programming behaviors and by creating buffers between activities that are difficult to coordinate; they also try to stabilize their environments. These efforts often produce desired consequences in the short term and then they prove harmful in the long term, as environments evolve despite organizations' efforts to stabilize them and programmed behaviors become increasingly inappropriate to changing threats and opportunities.

As well, a consistent theme emerging from these studies was that top managers developed views of their firms and their market environments that diverged greatly from what outsiders (and insiders) might have deemed realistic. One reason for this divergence was that the firms allocated information-gathering resources to the areas that appeared to them to be most important, and in so doing, they blinded themselves to environmental events that deviated from their managers' beliefs and expectations. A second reason was that the top managers had much more confidence in their personal experiences than in information coming from their subordinates. In every crisis we studied, the top managers received accurate warnings and diagnoses from some subordinates, but they paid no attention to these. Indeed, they sometimes laughed at them.

Hedberg and I eventually resolved our disagreement by concluding that both of us had been partly right. Of course, such an outcome may also have been a result of our friendship, which had grown much stronger over years of cooperation. We concluded that crises are indeed produced by organizations' environments, although not exactly in the way that Hedberg had conceived initially, and that crises are also produced by organizations themselves, but somewhat differently than I had thought at first.

* * *

Several events during the late 1970s suggested that I should revise my beliefs regarding what is real and what is not. When my chapter about the relations between organizations and their environments appeared in print, the adjacent chapter was one in which Roy Payne and Derek Pugh (1976) reviewed roughly 100 studies in which researchers had asked firms' members to characterize their firms' structures and cultures. They surmised that most people see their organizations inaccurately. Their data indicated that different members of an organization disagree so strongly with each other about almost every organizational property that it made no sense to talk about average perceptions and that members' perceptions of their organizations correlate very weakly with measurable characteristics of their organizations. In other words, the properties of organizations do not even have the support of consensus. Not only are organizational properties arcane, but also one might question whether organizations actually possess properties. Payne and Pugh did reassure me, however, when they reported that people know whether they are working in large organizations or small ones!

Another study that challenged my thinking was King's field experiment (1974), which implies that the consequences of actions may depend more strongly on the experimenters' theories than on their overt actions. On the surface, the study aimed at comparing two types of job redesign. However, the study had a 2×2 design in which their boss gave the plant managers different reasons for making the changes. The observed subsequent changes in productivity and absenteeism matched the reasons that the boss had stated, whereas the two types of job redesign yielded very similar levels of productivity and absenteeism. Thus, changes in actual work activities had tiny effects, but the different rationales for making changes seemed to induce quite different outcomes.

I gave a talk at a convention in which I contrasted subjective perceptions with objective data. Afterward, Karl Weick asked me: 'What if there are no objective data?' I found this question puzzling, almost incomprehensible. Nevertheless, having great respect for Weick's wisdom, I began to experiment with interpreting supposedly 'objective' data as arising from mental or social processes (Starbuck 2004).

* * *

An article by Peter Grinyer and David Norburn (1975) put a dent in my enthusiasm for strategic planning and also planted the seed of an idea about the evolution of social science. They examined the relationship of profitability to the use of strategic planning, and found that profitable business firms are nearly as likely to do no formal strategizing as to do it, and that the same is true of unprofitable firms. As I had been mindlessly assuming that strategizing helps firms increase their profits, this finding intrigued me, so I dug out as many studies as I could find of the relationships between profitability and the use of strategic planning. The oldest study, by Thune and House (1970), had reported a rather high, positive correlation. This discovery of a strong relationship had stimulated others to make additional studies, partly because these other researchers thought they could improve on the study by Thune and House. Over time, the reported correlations between profitability and the use of strategic planning had decreased toward zero. Eventually, in some studies that measured profitability with stock prices, the correlations varied around zero.

I wondered if I might possibly have noticed a widespread phenomenon: a social scientist reports finding a fairly strong relationship of some sort. This relationship might be quite general and robust, but it might instead result from methodological deficiencies or it might be a peculiarity of a specific source of data. The strong finding draws the attention of other researchers, who see deficiencies in the original study or have access to different data. They too find relationships, but weaker ones. Still more researchers appear, who try slightly different analytic methodology and different sources of data. These new findings indicate still weaker relationships. Eventually, as methodology evolves, the reported relationships hover around zero and researchers lose interest.

* * *

Studies by Tosi, Aldag, and Storey (1973) and by Downey, Hellriegel, and Slocum (1975) made me aware of another problem with spontaneous data, reinforced my skepticism about the usefulness of strategizing, and would lead a decade later to a research project on perceptual accuracy.

Lawrence and Lorsch had published a landmark study in 1967. After asking 'What types of organizations are most effective under different environmental conditions?', they (1967: 134) inferred that firms perform better when the firms' organizational properties align with the properties of their environments. However, their data were managers' perceptions and they had no other measures of either organizational properties or environmental properties. One could interpret Lawrence and Lorsch's findings as saying that managers are more likely to notice inconsistencies between firms' structures and their environments if the firms are performing poorly.

Lawrence and Lorsch had asked managers for their perceptions of 'environmental uncertainty'. Although Lawrence and Lorsch's theory said that environmental uncertainty involved several components, they had not asked about these components and they presented no evidence about the consistency among these components. Two groups of researchers tried to improve on Lawrence and Lorsch's methodology. Both groups asked middle and top managers to describe their uncertainty about their firms' markets and they not only asked about perceptions but also compared the perceptions with volatility indices calculated from the firms' financial reports and industry statistics. Correlating managers' perceptions with so-called 'objective' measures, both research groups found correlations that were near zero and negative more often than positive. Specifically, using data from 102 middle and top managers from twenty-two diverse firms, Tosi, Aldag, and Storey (1973) got correlations ranging from -0.29 to $+0.07$ between managers' perceptions of environmental uncertainty and volatility indices computed from industry and company data. Using data from fifty-one division heads in a large conglomerate, Downey, Hellriegel, and Slocum (1975) compared managers' environmental uncertainty and two components of environmental uncertainty with an index of volatility computed from industry statistics; the correlations ranged from -0.17 to $+0.06$. They also compared the components of environmental uncertainty with three other measures of managers' perceptions of their environments; these correlations ranged from -0.24 to $+0.21$. Furthermore,

Downey, Hellriegel, and Slocum (1977) found that managers' perceptions of their firms' environments correlate more strongly with the managers' personal characteristics than with the measured characteristics of the environments.

Tosi et al. and Downey et al. said that the low and erratic correlations in their studies might have arisen from poor questionnaires or poor objective measures of volatility. I, however, saw a very different interpretation: These studies might indicate that, on average, managers' perceptions of their environments' volatilities do not correlate with 'objective' measures of those volatilities. These studies also called my attention to the way both they and Lawrence and Lorsch had obtained their data—one method at one time. By including items in a single questionnaire or a single interview, researchers suggest to respondents that they ought to see relationships among these items; and by presenting items in nonrandom sequences, researchers imply how items relate. Only an insensitive respondent would ignore such strong hints. Indeed, respondents might conjecture that they ought to see relationships among items even if the items have random sequences. Moreover, respondents have almost certainly made sense of their worlds, even if they do not understand these worlds in some objective sense. For instance, managers' statements to Lawrence and Lorsch might be accurate descriptions that someone else could assess with independent measures, or they might be accurate descriptions of relationships that managers perceive, but these perceptions might diverge considerably from ones someone else could assess with independent measures (Starbuck 1985). Would anyone be surprised if managers perceive what makes sense to them, probably because their colleagues share these perceptions? Consensus about a belief may make it a fact for those who share it without making it a fact that others can reproduce.

* * *

Greenwald (1975) documented prejudice against null hypotheses through a survey of authors and reviewers for the *Journal of Personality and Social Psychology*. He also documented a few instances in which there have been 'epidemics of Type I error'—instances in which numerous studies disconfirmed null hypotheses that psychologists later judged to be true. Since statistical philosophy says that the probability of Type I error is small (0.01–0.05), the probability that a series of, say, ten studies would all make such errors ought to be very, very small.

However, it is not, and one explanation for why it is not very, very small could be that research is biased (Blaug 1980).

* * *

I spent most of my time from 1976 through 1979 giving feedback to authors of draft chapters for the *Handbook of Organizational Design*, an activity that began my sensitization to some subtle effects of linguistic practices on social science research. Since there were many chapters and I found myself writing similar comments over and over again, I began to collect examples of usages that seemed to distort meaning. Later, as a member of the editorial boards of several journals, I continued to compile such examples until I had many pages of them.

One insidious practice is the use of definite articles to describe representative instances, where indefinite articles would be accurate. Although my attempts to learn languages other than English have mainly shown me how incompetent I am at speaking them, these attempts have convinced me that definite and indefinite articles should have different meanings. In principle, a definite article (the) denotes a specific, nameable instance. 'The environment' means one specific environment, such as Indianapolis, the British sausage industry, or even, as one manager specified, above-ground Jewish burial on Long Island; and 'the organization' means one specific, nameable organization, such as Minnesota Mining or the University of Northern South Dakota. An indefinite article (a or an) designates a typical, nonspecific instance. Thus, 'an environment' means one typical environment, and 'an organization' means one typical organization.

Confusion of definite and indefinite articles causes substantive problems by allowing social scientists to manufacture generality from specific instances. For example, their penchant for saying 'the organization' has allowed organization theorists to gloss over the differences between organizations and to speak as if all organizations act the same way. Similarly, by saying 'the environment', organization theorists have understated the degrees to which environments are ambiguous, diverse, selected, and distinctive to specific organizations. Indeed, a proposition that raises no alarms when phrased in terms of 'the organization and its environment' may seem implausible when phrased as 'all organizations and all of the environments of each organization'. Note the misinterpretations that could arise from speaking of *the* theory of the firm, *the* regulatory process, or *the* decision-making process. Researchers should establish the homogeneity of social phenomena empirically rather than linguistically.

A related practice that erodes specificity more subtly and marginally but very consistently is the mixing of singulars and plurals, usually the use of singular nouns where plural nouns would be accurate. For example, authors have said 'the technical and social basis for wage attainments' and 'the properties of the environment of particular organizations'. Although it is very unlikely that wage attainments (plural) all have the same basis (singular), someone who says 'the technical and social basis for wage attainments' might well assume that a single explanation underlies all wage attainments. Likewise, although organizations develop environments that are partly unique, people who say 'the properties of the environment of particular organizations' might assume that different organizations all share the same environment. I have found that researchers do make such assumptions sometimes. I cannot say whether the language induces them to make these assumptions inadvertently, but mixtures of singulars and plurals often accompany unclear thought about whether data justify generalizations.

Two other practices that foster excessive generalization are using general nouns rather than specific ones and using different names for a single concept. For example, someone who has studied Happydale Nursing Home might describe it as a health care institution, implying that observations about Happydale generalize to other health care institutions. Someone who noticed a reduction in public dissent might describe the phenomenon as conflict reduction, implying that diverse types of conflict abated. As well, inconsistent terminology can blur the meaning of a concept. For example, one author equated 'goals' with 'outcomes', then with 'interests'. Another author equated 'consultant' with 'change agent', then with 'intervener', then with 'facilitator'. Yet another author equated 'causal texture of environment' with 'objective environment', and then with 'industry environment'. One reason to seek specificity and consistency is that social scientists too often try to endow their research with importance by using vague, pretentious terminology.

2.4 The 1980s

Publication of the *Handbook of Organizational Design* initiated what was, to me, an interesting phenomenon. The *Handbook* was supposed to stimulate a new approach to the study of organizations in which researchers would attempt to make changes in organizations and observe the consequences of those attempts. The *Handbook* was supposed to stimulate efforts to make organizations better—better by whatever criteria the designers might prefer. Precious little of either activity ensued. However, textbook publishers produced several new textbooks with titles that included the word 'design' even though they contained almost the same subject matter as the textbooks published several years earlier.

* * *

In 1981, I read a manuscript in which Brunsson (1982) argued that a perception held by only one person has the status of being subjective, and its effects are limited to that person's actions. On the other hand, he said, a widely shared perception acquires the status of being 'objective'; not only can it affect the actions of many people but also the actions of these people have the support of objective fact. Although this formulation seemed too radical, I could not deny that it meshed with some of my experience.

Around that same time, Meyer and Rowan (1977) interpreted the administrative structures of schools as facades that make schools appear legitimate. Administrative structures, they asserted, have negligible effects on what happens in classrooms, activities that have been much the same in many places and for many decades. Instead, administrative structures create the impression that schools look the way modern organizations ought to look, and thereby they reassure taxpayers that their schools are operating responsibly. If administrative structures have weak effects on classroom activities, they exert weak influence on the degrees to which students or teachers behave responsibly. Likewise, said Meyer and Rowan, hospitals and governmental agencies increase their chances of survival by mirroring rules valued by their societies.

This notion led Nystrom and me (1984) to survey a variety of ways in which business managers create facades. We argued that business managers conform to rules that their environments cherish and that such conformity may produce either desirable or undesirable consequences. Among these consequences has been some rather silly research by organization theorists who failed to recognize the superficiality of the behaviors or organizational properties they studied. Indeed, I have participated in such errors myself. Twice I have supervised doctoral students who attempted to analyze the letters to stockholders published in corporations' annual reports. Although signed by the corporations' presidents, some of these letters are written by public relations specialists, and the authors intend that these letters will make the current top managers look good. Thus, the letters mask some of the corporations' deficiencies and attempt to rationalize others.

* * *

Also around this time, I came to see the Aston studies as research about superficiality and facades. Asked to write a commentary on these studies, I dug into them in much greater detail than before (Starbuck 1981). I discovered that precise-looking numbers masked a morass of misleading labels and overlapping concepts, and that strong correlations had trivial meanings. For example, decoding their labels revealed that the researchers had discovered that autonomous organizations are less likely to receive instructions from above than are divisions of large organizations. A few findings that were not trivial had not replicated, probably because they had come from post hoc analyses. The most robust discoveries turned out to be ideas that had wide acceptance before the Aston studies began: (*a*) larger organizations are usually more bureaucratic than smaller ones, although possibly not proportionately more so; and (*b*) people who work in larger, more bureaucratic organizations espouse different values and have different perceptions than do people who work in smaller, less bureaucratic organizations. Whereas the Aston researchers set out to discover characteristics that generalize across all organizations, they actually showed that such characteristics are trite.

Many problems arose from the Aston researchers' focus on generalization, which induced them to ignore or deemphasize properties that make organizations distinctive. For example, the original Aston study examined eight autonomous organizations and thirty-eight subunits of organizations, and the researchers analyzed the data as if subunits were organizations. 'We included manufacturing firms that made strip steel, toys, double decker buses, chocolate bars, injection systems, and beer, and service organizations such as chain stores, municipal departments, transport companies, insurance companies, and a savings bank' (Pugh 1981: 141). Some of these organizations focused on local areas and others sold nationally. Further, the researchers carefully chose measures that would be equally meaningful in all organizations. 'It is the strength and the weakness of this project that no items were used unless they were applicable to all work organizations, whatever they did; several possible items of information had to be sacrificed to this end. Since the research strategy was to undertake a wide survey to set the guidelines, the result was superficiality and generality in the data' (Pugh et al. 1968: 69).

Their desire for generalization had the researchers comparing a savings bank with a steel mill while ignoring the fact that one safeguards money and makes loans while the other rolls hot steel. Most organizations exist in part because they perform specific functions that other nearby organizations do not perform, and some organizations achieve unusual success by performing functions that no others perform. By omitting data about organizations' distinctiveness, the researchers excluded the data that could show why organizations mattered. The properties that all organizations possess are primarily ones that have weak effects on organizations' core functions, such as variables describing housekeeping activities (record keeping, accounting) or variables relating to administrative facades.

As well, the Aston researchers' findings depended very strongly on assumptions embedded in their measures, and their reports gave no indication that they realized how strongly these assumptions had affected their findings. Many of their findings had commonsense interpretations that were very different from the meanings implied by the names the researchers had given to variables (Starbuck 1981). The researchers created variables by aggregating scores on several questionnaire items, and variables with different names sometimes included identical items of data. One result was correlations between variables that were due entirely to the researchers' methodology. Indeed, the Aston group's findings were overwhelmingly findings about the researchers themselves—their prior beliefs, their decisions about methodology, and their acts of labeling and interpretation.

If the Aston studies had been conducted poorly, one might blame their deficiencies on the researchers' errors, insensitivity, or incompetence. However, the studies were carefully designed by excellent researchers, who were later seen as a Who's Who of British organizational research. As well, many of the Aston group were my dear friends, people I admired for their high standards, intellect, and sincerity. Indeed, their methodology was widely admired and their articles appeared in the most prestigious journals and were widely cited by other studies and textbooks. Hence, I saw these studies as an idealization of a methodological approach and their deficiencies as attributes of this approach.

*   *   *

Another methodological lesson came in the form of an amusing story told by Kenneth Pelletier, a doctor from Berkeley, California. Pelletier's story demonstrated to me the uncertainty associated with inferring causation based on aggregate data that do not describe causal processes. He said he wanted to investigate how it is that people live to be 140 years old, so he applied for a federal government grant for this purpose. To generate hypotheses for his grant application, he identified four societies in which it was supposedly quite common for people to live to 140 years of age, and then he looked for common properties among these societies.

He could quickly rule out climate because the societies live in very different climates. He could also rule out medical care because none of the societies has any of that. Still, he did spot five properties that the four societies share.

Firstly, they are vegetarian—although not necessarily by choice. They have little access to meat.

Secondly, in all of these societies, everyone works hard throughout their lives. No one can retire. People must work to eat.

Thirdly, these societies exhibit strong social solidarity. If two people are living together and one dies, neighbors make the survivor a part of their family.

Fourthly, about once a week, everybody in a village gets together and gets blind, roaring drunk. Pelletier speculated that this alleviates stress and fosters solidarity, while the social context and periodicity make alcoholism unlikely.

Lastly, people in these societies continue to have sexual intercourse at least to the age of 120.

*   *   *

As the editor of a special issue of a journal, Dick Cyert asked me to review the progress that had occurred in computer simulation in the ten years since Dutton and I had published our anthology. I was quite surprised to find that simulation had not continued to become more widely used and that several research domains that had earlier been enthusiastic about simulation had abandoned it (Starbuck 1983*a*). The few simulation articles published in 1980 and 1981 were no more rigorous or polished than those published one or two decades earlier. Often, researchers had published articles outlining models that they said they intended to build, but no articles reporting the results of their work. Efforts to predict urban development, geographic diffusion, and traffic flows had so greatly disappointed researchers that they abandoned simulation; their simulations had shown the researchers that it was not merely a lack of data and computing capacity that had prevented them from making accurate predictions but a lack of adequate theories. Only economists had continued to develop simulations, but their simulation efforts had yielded unconvincing results. Of four projects by teams of economists to forecast macroeconomic trends, three had proven distinctly less accurate than linear extrapolation and the fourth had been only about as accurate as linear extrapolation (Elliott 1973).

* * *

Someone sent me an address that Hayek (1975) made when he won the Nobel Prize in Economic Sciences. Hayek protested that social scientists focus on phenomena for which they have quantitative measures, and that they try to use causal reasoning where they lack adequate understanding of causal processes. Quantitative measures describe rather limited aspects of phenomena; people can rarely know or measure the determinants of outcomes of complex phenomena; the partial-derivative thinking that pervades theorizing assumes that just a few effects interact weakly. One result, Hayek (1975) alleged, is that economists have developed simple theories that greatly understate the complexity of economic phenomena and consequently generate policies that make economic problems worse. In particular, the economic policies that economists developed to remedy unemployment, argued Hayek, create large-scale unemployment whenever inflation stops accelerating.

* * *

Invited to write a chapter about theory building in organizational behavior, I took the opportunity to investigate my earlier conjectures about successive research studies evolving toward zero correlations (Webster and Starbuck 1988). My coauthor, Jane Webster, dug up the histories of nine relationships that had long been important in industrial psychology, a sister field of organizational behavior. Since these relationships had attracted research for many years, we expected that studies of them might show constant or increasing strength over time—increasing strength as researchers developed better measures, obtained more appropriate data, and applied more controls.

Figure 2.1 shows the correlations of job satisfaction with absenteeism, of job satisfaction with job performances, and of subordinates' perceptions of leaders with the leaders' intelligence. Figure 2.2 shows the percentage improvements in job performance following two types of interventions—goal setting and behavior modification. Five of the nine relationships we examined had trended toward zero over time— the correlations of job satisfaction with absenteeism, the correlations of turnover with realistic job previews, the correlations of turnover with job enrichment, the performance improvements with behavior modification, and the correlations of observed results with Fiedler's contingency theory of leadership. Three relationships had remained approximately constant for many years—the correlations of job satisfaction with job performances, the performance improvements with goal setting, and the correlations of subordinates' perceptions of leaders with the leaders' intelligence. Measures of only one relationship had increased, but this increase was entirely due to the very oldest study, which had reported a very weak relationship. Furthermore, this relationship was trivial: It said some of the people who state in private that they intend to quit their jobs actually do quit.

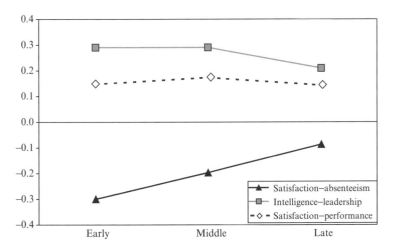

Figure 2.1 Mean correlations over time

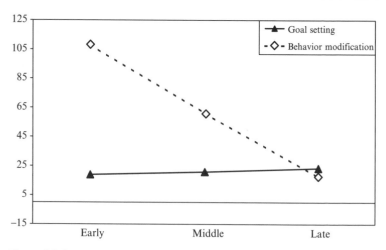

Figure 2.2 Percentage improvements with interventions over time

Webster and I could imagine five reasons why none of these effect sizes had risen noticeably after the first years: Firstly, researchers may be clinging to incorrect theories despite disconfirming evidence (Staw 1976). This would be more likely to happen where studies' findings allow diverse interpretations. For example, absolutely small correlations nurture equivocality by making it appear that random noise dominates any systematic relationships and that undiscovered or uninteresting influences exert much more effect than the known influences.

Secondly, researchers may be continuing to elaborate traditional methods of information gathering after these stop generating additional information. For example, researchers developed very good leadership questionnaires during the early 1950s. Perhaps these early questionnaires picked up all the information about leadership that questionnaires can gather. Thus, subsequent questionnaires may not have represented robust improvements; they may merely have mistaken sampling variations for generalities.

Thirdly, most studies may fail to take advantage of the genuinely useful information produced by the best studies. This would be unlikely as a sole explanation because research journals receive wide distribution and researchers can easily read reports of others' projects. However, retrospective interpretations of random variations may obscure real information in clouds of ad hoc rationalizations, so the consumers of research may have difficulty distinguishing real information from false.

Fourthly, the studies obtaining the largest effect sizes may do so for idiosyncratic or unknown reasons, and thus produce no generalizable knowledge. Because very few studies report correlations above 0.5, almost all studies leave much scope for misattribution and misinterpretation, and published interpretations are biased by researchers' tendencies to attribute observed phenomena to relationships they expected to see (Snyder 1981; Faust 1984; Klayman and Ha 1987). Research reports generally provide too little information about studied sites, subjects, or situations to enable later research to build upon prior findings (Orwin and Cordray 1985), and researchers may not even be aware of the variables that influence their findings (Latham, Erez, and Locke 1988).

Lastly, people's characteristics and behaviors may change faster than social scientists' theories and measures improve. Stagner (1982) argued that the context of industrial–organizational psychology has changed considerably over the years: the economy has shifted from production to service industries; jobs have evolved from heavy labor to cognitive functions; employees' education levels have risen; and legal requirements have multiplied and changed, especially with respect to discrimination. For instance, in the USA employment in government, finance, and professional services rose from 17 percent in 1950 to 46 percent in 2001. The fastest-growing occupations have been professional and technical workers and managers and administrators. Managers' years of education correlate with their ideas about proper leadership (Haire, Ghiselli, and Porter 1966), and education alters subordinates' concepts of proper leadership (Dreeben 1968; Kunda 1992). In 1950, 11 percent of adults had less than five years of schooling and 33 percent had completed twelve years of schooling; by 1998, only 1.6 percent had less than five years and 83 percent had completed twelve years. Haire, Ghiselli, and Porter also attributed 25 percent of the variance in managers' leadership beliefs to national differences. As people move around, either between countries or within a large country, they break down the differences between regions and create new beliefs that blend beliefs that were once distinct. Cummings and Schmidt (1972) conjectured plausibly that beliefs about proper leadership vary with industrialization, and globalization has been spreading industrialization around the world.

43

Transoceanic travel more than tripled from 1985 to 1998, and transoceanic communications multiplied twenty-eight times from 1986 to 1997. Thus, the practices that constitute effective leadership have been evolving even as researchers have been attempting to develop understanding of what constitutes effective leadership.

Webster proposed that industrial–organizational psychology might be producing poor research results because it lacked paradigm consensus. Kuhn (1962) had argued that scientific progress alternates between brief spurts of rapid change and long periods of consensus building. Had industrial–organizational psychology been fallow during a long period of consensus building? Did industrial–organizational psychologists exhibit consensus? Various reviews had suggested that industrial–organizational psychologists disagree with each other about the substance of theories. Might industrial–organizational psychologists have low paradigm consensus but be employing quantitative, large-sample research methods that presume high paradigm consensus?

We looked at three measures of paradigm consensus in journals: citing half-lives, percentages of references to the same journal, and numbers of references per article. Figure 2.3 shows citing half-lives for journals in sociology, organizational behavior, psychology, industrial–organizational psychology, chemistry, physics, management, and management information systems. Citing half-lives, the median ages of the references in journals, indicate the speed with which concepts evolve. Figure 2.4 shows the percentages of references to the same journal; high percentages suggest higher paradigm consensus. Figure 2.5 shows numbers of references per article; numerous references may also suggest higher paradigm consensus. According to these measures, industrial–organizational psychology looked much like organizational behavior and psychology in general. This was no surprise, of course. Industrial–organizational psychology also looked different from management information systems, which appeared to lack paradigm consensus and to be changing rapidly.

To our astonishment, industrial–organizational psychology did not look very different from chemistry and physics, two fields that were widely perceived as having high paradigm consensus and as making rapid progress. We speculated that industrial–organizational psychology might differ significantly from the physical sciences in paradigms' content, however. Physical science paradigms evidently embraced both substance and methodology,

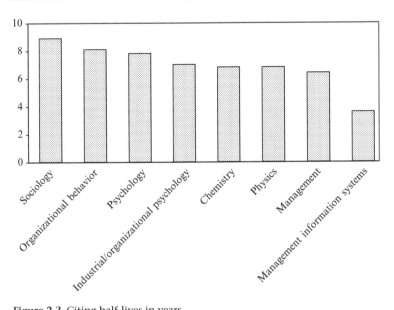

Figure 2.3 Citing half-lives in years

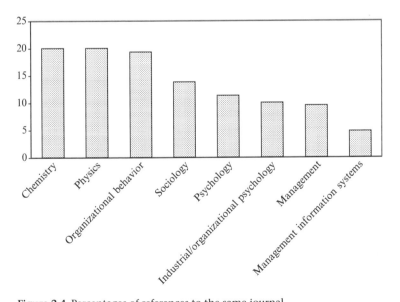

Figure 2.4 Percentages of references to the same journal

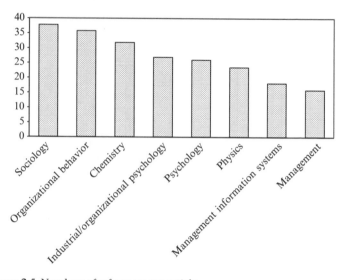

Figure 2.5 Numbers of references per article

whereas industrial–organizational psychology paradigms strongly emphasized methodology and paid little attention to substance. Industrial–organizational psychologists were acting as if they did not agree with each other concerning the substance of human behavior, although Webster and I believed that this lack of substantive consensus was probably superficial.

Our measures of consensus made no distinction between substantive consensus and methodological consensus. On one hand, Garvey, Lin, and Nelson (1970) had inferred that editorial practices in the social sciences placed more emphasis on methodology than did those in the physical sciences. On the other hand, when Campbell, Daft, and Hulin had asked American industrial–organizational psychologists to recommend 'the major research needs' of their field, 105 psychologists had offered 146 suggestions, of which 106 were unique. Campbell, Daft, and Hulin (1982: 71) inferred, 'The field does not have very well worked out ideas about what it wants to do. There was relatively little consensus about the relative importance of substantive issues.' Therefore, Webster and I speculated that industrial–organizational psychologists might be disagreeing about the relative importance of substantive issues but be agreeing about proper research methodology.

Indeed, industrial–organizational psychologists might be emphasizing methodology and de-emphasizing substance because they did not trust their inferences from empirical evidence. They ought to distrust their inferences, we proposed, because their methodology generates multitudes of small, but statistically significant, relationships that are substantively insignificant.

Induction requires distinguishing meaningful relationships (signals) in the midst of an obscuring background of confounding relationships (noise). The weak and meaningless or substantively secondary correlations in the background make induction untrustworthy. In many tasks, people can distinguish weak signals against rather strong background noise. The reason is that both the signals and the background noise match familiar patterns. For example, a driver traveling to a familiar destination focuses on landmarks that experience has shown to be relevant. People have trouble making such distinctions where signals and noise look much alike or where signals and noise have unfamiliar characteristics. For example, a driver traveling a new road to a new destination is likely to have difficulty spotting landmarks and turns on a recommended route.

Social science research has the latter characteristics. This activity is called research because its outputs are unknown; and the signals and noise look a lot alike in that both have systematic components and both contain components that vary erratically. Therefore, researchers rely upon statistical techniques to distinguish signals from noise. However, these techniques assume: (*a*) that the so-called random errors really do cancel each other out so that their average values are close to zero; and (*b*) that the so-called random errors in different variables are uncorrelated. These are very strong assumptions because they presume that the researchers' hypotheses encompass absolutely all of the systematic effects in the data, including effects that the researchers have not foreseen or measured. When these assumptions are not met, the statistical techniques tend to mistake noise for signal, and to attribute more importance to the researchers' hypotheses than they deserve.

I remembered what Ames and Reiter (1961) had said about how easy it is for macroeconomists to discover statistically significant correlations that have no substantive significance, and I could see five reasons why a similar phenomenon might occur with cross-sectional data. Firstly, a few broad characteristics of people and social systems pervade social science data—examples being sex, age, intelligence, social class, income, education, or organization size. Such characteristics correlate with many behaviors and with each other. Secondly, researchers' decisions about how to treat data can create correlations between variables. For example, when the Aston researchers used factor analysis to create aggregate variables, they implicitly determined the correlations among these aggregate variables. Thirdly, so-called 'samples' are frequently not random, and many of them are complete subpopulations—say, every employee of a company—even though study after study has turned up evidence that people who live close together, who work together, or who socialize together tend to have more attitudes, beliefs, and behaviors in common than do people who are far apart physically and socially. Fourthly, some studies obtain data from respondents at one time and through one method. By including items in a single questionnaire or interview, researchers suggest to respondents that relationships exist among these items. Lastly, most researchers are intelligent people who are living successful lives. They are likely to have some intuitive ability to predict the behaviors of people and of social systems. They are much more likely to formulate hypotheses that accord with their intuition than ones that violate it; they are quite likely to investigate correlations and differences that deviate from zero; and they are less likely than chance would imply to observe correlations and differences near zero.

Webster and I hypothesized that statistical tests with a null hypothesis of no correlation are biased toward statistical significance. Webster culled through *Administrative Science Quarterly*, the *Academy of Management Journal*, and the *Journal of Applied Psychology* seeking matrices of correlations. She tabulated only complete matrices of correlations in order to observe the relations among all of the variables that the researchers perceived when drawing inductive inferences, not only those variables that researchers actually included in hypotheses. Of course, some researchers probably gathered data on additional variables beyond those published, and then omitted these additional variables because they correlated very weakly with the dependent variables. We estimated that 64 percent of the correlations in our data were associated with researchers' hypotheses.

Figure 2.6 shows the distributions of 14,897 correlations. In all three journals, both the mean correlation and the median correlation were close to $+0.09$ and the distributions of correlations were very similar. Finding significant correlations is absurdly easy in this popu-

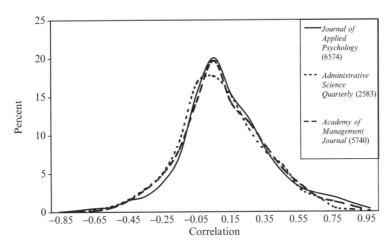

Figure 2.6 Correlations reported in three journals

lation of variables, especially when researchers make two-tailed tests with a null hypothesis of no correlation. Choosing two variables utterly at random, a researcher has 2-to-1 odds of finding a significant correlation on the first try, and 24-to-1 odds of finding a significant correlation within three tries (also see Hubbard and Armstrong 1992). Furthermore, the odds are better than 2-to-1 that an observed correlation will be positive, and positive correlations are more likely than negative ones to be statistically significant. Because researchers gather more data when they are getting small correlations, studies with large numbers of observations exhibit slightly less positive bias. The mean correlation in studies with fewer than seventy observations is about twice the mean correlation in studies with over 180 observations.

The main inference I drew from these statistics was that the social sciences are drowning in statistically significant but meaningless noise. Because the differences and correlations that social scientists test have distributions quite different from those assumed in hypothesis tests, social scientists are using tests that assign statistical significance to confounding background relationships. Because social scientists equate statistical significance with meaningful relationships, they often mistake confounding background relationships for theoretically important information. One result is that social science research creates a cloud of statistically significant differences and correlations that not only have no real meaning but also impede scientific progress by obscuring the truly meaningful relationships.

Suppose that roughly 10 percent of all observable relations could be theoretically meaningful and that the remaining 90 percent either have no meanings or can be deduced as implications of the key 10 percent. However, we do not know now which relations constitute the key 10 percent, and so our research resembles a search through a haystack in which we are trying to separate needles from more numerous straws. Now suppose that we adopt a search method that makes almost every straw look very much like a needle and that turns up thousands of apparent needles annually; 90 percent of these apparent needles are actually straws, but we have no way of knowing which ones. Next, we fabricate a theory that 'explains' these apparent needles. Some of the propositions in our theory are likely to be correct, merely by chance; but many, many more propositions are incorrect or misleading in that they describe straws. Even if this theory were to account rationally for all of the needles that we have supposedly discovered in the past, which is extremely unlikely, the theory has very little chance of making highly accurate predictions about the consequences of our actions unless the theory itself acts as a powerful self-fulfilling prophecy (Eden and Ravid 1982). Our theory would make some correct predictions, of course, because with so many correlated variables, even a completely false theory would have a reasonable chance of generating predictions that come true. Thus, we dare not even take correct predictions as dependable evidence of our theory's correctness (Deese 1972: 61–67).

*   *   *

I read two relevant articles in the mid-1980s. Lovell analyzed how data mining affects statistical tests. Researchers often make calculations regarding many different statistical models, and statistical software generally offers ways to try many alternative models automatically (e.g. stepwise regression). Further, researchers often fail to report calculations that they deemed to yield unsatisfactory fits. Reported or not, each additional calculation increases the probability of obtaining an apparently significant result by chance. Lovell (1983: 1) observed, 'When a data miner uncovers t-statistics that appear significant at the 0.05 level by running a large number of alternative regressions on the same body of data, the probability of a Type I error of rejecting the null hypothesis when it is true is much greater than the claimed 5%.' He proceeded to show that searches for explanatory variables typically yield impressive multiple correlations and high levels of significance, and he suggested various corrective measures including the one of not claiming that analyses generalize beyond the specific sample analyzed.

Peach and Webb argued that statistical analyses afford inadequate bases for selecting among alternative economic models. They (1983: 697) showed 'that almost any regression equation using the kinds of time series variables typically included in macroeconomic models...is likely to have a good statistical fit to actual data points—that is, as good as regression estimates cited as evidence supporting theoretical propositions in the literature'. They proceeded to assemble 300 hypothetical 'models' by selecting fifty random combinations of a dependent variable and three independent variables and analyzing these with three types of linear models and two time spans of data. Depending on the model and time span of data, 64–71 percent of the independent variables had 'statistically significant' coefficients. With a simple linear model, 64 percent of the combinations of variables had R^2s over 0.99 and 94 percent had R^2s over 0.95. When variables were converted to first differences, which greatly reduces autocorrelation, 32 percent of the combinations of variables had R^2s over 0.60 and 10 percent had R^2s over 0.80. When lagged values of the dependent variable appeared on the right side of the equation, 80–90 percent of the combinations of variables had R^2s over 0.99.

* * *

In the mid-1980s, I moved to New York University, where I jumped at the chance to teach forecasting. I had a fantasy that forecasters might actually know, better than other people, how to foretell the future and I was curious about the nature of this expertise. This teaching experience altered my views of statistical analyses and empirical research generally (Pant and Starbuck 1990).

Possibly, the most profound lesson that forecasting taught me was one that I should have anticipated: Theories that are useful for making statements about the future are different from theories that are useful for making statements about the past. Analyses of past events tend to favor complex and subtle explanations and elegant techniques that make strong assumptions about the properties of data. Why not? Since researchers know what has happened, they know a good deal about the properties of data and they can avoid theoretical conjectures that are blatantly inconsistent with the data. However, complex explanations and elegant techniques have consistently disappointed forecasters. Analytic techniques that promise to extract more information from data tend to mistake noise for information. They perform best for stable situations that contain little random noise—where any method would be accurate—and they perform most poorly where situations are changing rapidly or where random noise is large. For example, to predict that a trend will change direction, one needs to use a technique that reacts strongly and nonlinearly to new information. However, a computation scheme has no way to distinguish whether an unexpected new event is idiosyncratic or it is the first sign of a changed trend. Because trends change infrequently and idiosyncratic events are frequent, it has turned out in practice that predictions of trend changes have nearly always been wrong. Likewise, subtle relationships seen in past data rarely recur with sufficient force to produce discernible effects in future data. In fact, the high autocorrelations that make it possible to predict future events accurately over the short run also create spurious correlations between time series that foster incorrect inferences about causal relations.

For example, since the 1950s, macroeconomists have invested enormous resources in trying to create complex, mathematical, statistically estimated theories that predict short-run phenomena well. The teams that developed these models included some of the world's most respected economists, and they spent hundreds of man-years. They used elegant statistical methodology. They did not lack financial or computation resources, for the US government spent many millions of dollars for data gathering and research grants. Major industrial firms pay large sums for the predictions generated by these models. Therefore, these models represent superior efforts in economic or social forecasting.

Elliott (1973) tested the predictive accuracies of four of the best-known macroeconomic forecasting models. Of course, the model builders had presented evidence of their predictive accuracies, but these claims of accuracy had come from 'predicting' the same data that the model builders had used to estimate the models' coefficients, and each of the four models had been fitted to data from a different period. Elliott fitted all four models to data from the same period, and then measured their accuracies in predicting subsequent events. Three models turned out to be as accurate as the hypothesis that the economy would remain unchanged for the next three months. The simplest model, which was the most accurate, was as accurate as the hypothesis that 'the trend during the last three months will continue through the next three months'.

Two other lessons that forecasting taught me concerned the deficiencies of squared-error statistics, which are the statistics that most social scientists use most of the time. Firstly, least-squares regression produces unreliable results from noisy data. Regression weights may actually contain less information than merely knowing whether predictor variables relate positively or negatively to a dependent variable, so forecasters may make less accurate predictions if they use regression to infer that a dependent variable correlates more strongly with one predictor variable than with another. Secondly, if researchers use squared errors to measure fits to historical data and forecasting accuracies, better fitting models do not predict better, even in the very short run. However, better fitting models would predict better if researchers would replace squared-error criteria with more reliable measures of fit.

I first encountered these problems when reading about efforts to predict the outcomes of employee selection and college admissions. There has been an old tradition of evaluating applicants for jobs or for college admission by checking off their characteristics on lists. Evaluators then added up the numbers of checkmarks to determine applicants' suitability, which implicitly gave each item equal weight. For example, the earliest college entrance exams assigned equal weight to each question. The items on entrance exams or employment forms did not come from statistical studies but from a priori assumptions.

During the 1950s, psychometricians began to advocate the use of squared-error regression to assign weights to items (Perloff 1951). The psychometricians argued that regression would assign higher weights to items that are more important and would eliminate redundant or uninformative items. Statistical theory asserted that regression weights would minimize prediction errors. To the surprise of many, however, two decades of experience showed that regression weights made predictions less accurate. Prediction scores computed with regression-derived weights correlated less highly with students' or employees' actual performances than had scores generated by equally weighted a priori items (Boyce 1955; Lawshe and Schucker 1959; Wesman and Bennett 1959).

Schmidt, Claudy, and Dorans and Dragow used computer simulation to investigate this phenomenon. They assumed an ideal situation—perfect Normal distributions and independent variables with no measurement errors. Schmidt (1971) examined sample sizes ranging from 25 to 1,000. With ten independent variables, regression was inferior to equal weights unless there were more than 100–200 observations. Furthermore, even with samples of 1,000, regression coefficients were only slightly superior to equal weights. Claudy (1972) examined sample sizes ranging from 20 to 160 and one to five independent variables. With independent variables that intercorrelated between 0 and 0.4, regression was inferior to equal weights for all sample sizes. Even with the largest samples (160), regression was either inferior or only slightly superior to equal weights for over half of the tested populations. Dorans and Drasgow (1978) compared six methods, and found that equal weighting outscored the other five methods when making predictions about new samples from the same population. Equal weighting had as high cross-sample validity for small samples as for large ones, whereas the other methods had lower validities for smaller samples. Regression drew the least reliable inferences from small samples and the most reliable inferences from large samples.

Einhorn and Hogarth (1975) used algebra to compare regression with equal weights, and they introduced another factor—the magnitude of the multiple correlation. They concluded: (*a*) over wide ranges of sample sizes and numbers of independent variables, there is little difference between regression weights and equal weights; (*b*) equal weights are more reliable than regression weights when samples are small, when multiple correlations are not high, or when independent variables intercorrelate. With ten independent variables and multiple correlations below 0.5, samples might have to exceed 400 before regression weights become as reliable as equal weights. Einhorn and Hogarth's analyses assumed perfect Normal distributions; equal weights would have even greater advantages relative to regression weights if the data are not perfectly Normal.

Thus, these theoretical studies said that researchers need at least several hundred degrees of freedom in order for coefficients computed by regression analyses to enable more reliable predictions than do equal weights. With statistical distributions that closely resemble Normal distributions, independent variables that do not correlate with each other, and a multiple correlation over 0.5, 200 degrees of freedom might be sufficient. With a multiple correlation below 0.5, 400 degrees of freedom might be necessary. Also unsettling, I thought, is the weak improvement that regression is capable of making. Even with very large samples of 1,000 to 5,000, regression coefficients are only slightly better than equal weights.

Squared-error regression requires large samples because squared errors give great influence to observations that lie far from regression lines. These outlying observations represent low-probability events that are unlikely to recur in other samples drawn from the same populations, so sample idiosyncrasies have strong effects. Regression coefficients reflect the idiosyncrasies of the samples used to compute them, and these samples are very unlikely to exhibit similar idiosyncrasies to the samples for which predictions are made. Sample idiosyncrasies also have strong effects because the criterion function—the sum of the squared errors—makes weak distinctions near its minimum. That is, the criterion function is flat and changes rather little when the estimated coefficients change a lot, making coefficient estimates volatile.

Theoretical analyses that assume stable Normal distributions assert that a model's squared-error fit with historical data should predict its squared-error forecasting accuracy. Yet, a statistical model that fits historical data more closely in terms of squared errors does not make more accurate forecasts in terms of squared errors. Indeed, knowing a model's squared-error fit with historical data can be worse than knowing nothing whatever about its predictive potential (Pant and Starbuck 1990).

When averaged across many time series, squared errors emphasize the highly variable series. When applied to a single series, squared errors emphasize the outlying data. Because outliers have low probabilities, squared errors place importance on the low-probability events. Thus, squared-error measures are unreliable and the errors in forecasts may diverge strikingly from errors found when fitting models to historical data.

* * *

During the 1960s, one of my colleagues at Purdue University had proposed that I join Sigma Xi, an organization of research scientists. Consequently, my reading material has included *American Scientist*, a periodical that encompasses the biological, physical, and social sciences. This reading disclosed that bioecologists had been debating whether to replace null hypotheses. Connor and Simberloff (1983, 1986) argued that interactions within ecological communities make statistical tests based on simple null hypotheses too unrealistic. They proposed that bioecologists replace null hypotheses with 'null models', which they (1986: 160) defined as follows: 'A null model is an attempt to generate the distribution of values for the variable of interest in the absence of a putative causal process.' That is, one uses a 'null model' to generate a statistical distribution, and then one asks whether the observed data have high or low probabilities according to this distribution.

For example, different islands in the Galapagos hold different numbers of species of land birds: these numbers might reflect competition between species, physical differences among the islands, or vegetation differences. Using a 'null model' that ignored competition between species, Connor and Simberloff (1983) estimated the statistical distributions of the numbers of species pairs on islands in the Galapagos. Their estimates assumed that each island held the number of species observed on it and that each species inhabited as many islands as observed, but that species were otherwise distributed randomly and independently. All the observed numbers of species pairs fell within two standard deviations of the means in the distributions implied by this null model, and most observations were quite close to the expected values. Hence, Connor and Simberloff inferred that competition between species had had little effect on the numbers of species of Galapagos land birds.

Not surprisingly, some bioecologists voiced strong reservations about 'null models' (Harvey et al. 1983). Among several points of contention, Gilpin and Diamond (1984) argued: (*a*) that 'null models' are not truly null because they make implicit assumptions; and (*b*) that they are difficult to reject because fitting coefficients to data removes randomness. Gilpin and Diamond do have a point, in that describing such models as 'null' might create false expectations regarding the absence of assumptions. Connor and Simberloff's 'null model', for instance, took as premises the observed numbers of species on each island and the observed numbers of islands inhabited by each species. These observations implicitly incorporate information about some physical and vegetation differences among the islands, and Gilpin and Diamond noted that these numbers might reflect competition between species as well. On the other hand, Connor and Simberloff (1986: 161) pointed out that scientists can choose null models that virtually guarantee their own rejection: 'For this null model, and for null models in general, if one is unwilling to make assumptions to account for structure in the data that can reasonably be attributed to causal processes not under investigation, then posing and rejecting null hypotheses will be trivially easy and uninteresting.'

Computers play a key role in debates about null hypotheses. The distributions computed by Connor and Simberloff would have required superhuman effort before 1950. One of statisticians' original reasons for using point null hypotheses was algebraic feasibility. Because they had to manipulate statistical distributions algebraically, they built analytic rationales around algebraically amenable distributions. Computers give researchers means to generate statistical distributions that represent assumptions that are more complicated. It is no longer necessary to use the distributions published in textbooks.

2.5 The 1990s

During the late 1980s and early 1990s, one of my friends made two studies that failed to reject null hypotheses. In the first study, he devoted much effort to formulating an a priori theory about the phenomena based on published research. He felt strong commitments to this theory; he tried very hard to confirm it; and he ended up rejecting it only after months of reanalysis. He recoded his data several times and he tried alternative statistical tests. Eventually, he realized that the lack of clear differences was itself very interesting. His research compared public reports made by companies in trouble with the equivalent reports made by companies that were doing well, and his analyses suggested that the two sets of reports looked nearly identical. Thus, companies in trouble might be striving to make it appear that they were doing well. Further, several other researchers had been drawing data from companies' public reports and his study was suggesting that researchers should be suspicious about these data.

He sent his study to *Administrative Science Quarterly* (*ASQ*) and the reviewers asked him to revise it by 'testing' a posteriori hypotheses that the reviewers themselves proposed. The reviewers advised him to describe his study falsely. They told him to portray their proposals as hypotheses that he had formulated a priori; and they told him to portray his original null hypothesis falsely as an alternative a priori hypothesis. In fact, the reviewers repeated this behavior three times. Three times they asked him to 'test' additional hypotheses that they themselves proposed; three times he did as they asked; and three times his statistical tests failed to confirm their hypotheses. Finally, after three revisions, the editor rejected his manuscript.

He then submitted his manuscript to the *Academy of Management Journal*, and editorial events there replicated those at *ASQ*. Three times, the reviewers asked him to 'test' additional hypotheses that they themselves proposed; three times he did as they asked; and three times his statistical tests failed to confirm their hypotheses. Again, after three revisions, the editor rejected his manuscript.

He then sent his manuscript to the *Journal of Management Studies*, which asked me to review it. I recommended a drastic pruning. The numerous hypotheses proposed by previous reviewers had created a morass of confusion and ambiguity. By the time the author had finished explaining a score of hypotheses, and made statistical tests of their permutations, the basic point had become invisible. The author never made the revision I requested. He has locked the study in a file drawer labeled 'Disaster Paper'.

In the second study, this man started by proposing two a priori theories and then he revised these theories to accommodate critiques by many colleagues. As a result, the stated hypotheses had received rather general endorsement. Again, he felt strong commitments to his a priori theories; he tried very hard to confirm them; and he ended up rejecting them only after months of reanalysis. However, because his first study had met such resistance, he did not even attempt to describe the second study forthrightly as a test of two alternative theories against a null hypothesis: Instead, convinced that journals do not want honest reports, he wrote his report as if he had entertained three alternative theories from the outset. However, this study too elicited rejections.

In their responses to both studies, reviewers complained that the studies had failed to reject the null hypotheses, not because the alternative hypotheses are wrong, but because the basic data are too noisy, because the researcher used poor measures, or because the stated hypotheses poorly represented valid general theories. The reviewers' complaints were not credible, however. In the first study, the researcher reprocessed the raw data several times, both to improve the accuracy of measures and to meet the objections of reviewers. He also tested, but did not confirm, hypotheses that the reviewers themselves had proposed. In the second study, before gathering data, the researcher had sought extensive input from colleagues so as to make his hypotheses as defensible as possible. Thus, the reviewers seemed to be giving methodological reasons for rejecting manuscripts that contradicted their substantive beliefs (Mahoney 1977).

After-the-fact reflection about both studies suggested that the null hypotheses made very significant statements about the phenomena. That is, after one accepts (albeit reluctantly) the idea that the null hypotheses described the data quite accurately, one can see the phenomena quite differently than past research had done and one can see opportunities for innovative research. Thus, the reviewers rejected innovative work that could have had profound implications.

At this point, my friend shifted to another data-gathering method that allowed him to obtain sample sizes of about 2,500. He did this because, as he put it, 'If someone sneezes, it's statistically significant.' He then submitted a third study to the *Academy of Management Journal*, which rejected it. However, my friend refused to accept this rejection. He revised the manuscript according to the reviewers' advice and resubmitted it. This time he received an invitation to revise the manuscript and again he revised the manuscript according to the reviewers' advice and resubmitted it. At that point, he received a letter asking for minor revisions. A committee chose his paper as the best one published by that journal that year. He said, 'I succumbed to doing how most people do papers. It's an iterative process. Hypothesize, crunch, hypothesize, crunch.' I asked him how he felt about the result. He replied, 'Do I believe what I found? I don't think so.'

* * *

Hedberg invited me to speak at a conference that would be devoted to 'knowledge-intensive firms'. I liked the idea of a trip to Sweden and the chance to visit Hedberg. However, I had no idea what a knowledge-intensive firm might be, so I asked several colleagues what the term connoted to them. Each offered a very different definition, and after several weeks, I still had no idea what a knowledge-intensive firm might be. I decided that I had better go look at some. I thought of organizations that focused on the sale of expertise of various kinds—consultants, researchers, analyzers, technical experts—and I went to visit eight firms (Starbuck 1992*a*).

I found that experts in these firms were all doing much the same things. They gathered information through interviews or reading, they analyzed and interpreted this information, and they made written and oral reports to clients and colleagues. The similarities were striking across people, sites, and projects. Yet, the experts themselves described their activities diversely. Some said that they were applying old knowledge to new problems, others that they were creating new knowledge, and still others that they were preserving knowledge that already existed. Some experts said that they were preserving information for clients who had difficulty retaining it. Experts who saw themselves as producing new knowledge emphasized the recency or originality of their data and the differences between their findings and those of predecessors. By contrast, experts who saw themselves mainly as applying existing knowledge to current problems emphasized the continuity over time of knowledge and its meaning, and they deemphasized the innovative quality of their reasoning.

These descriptions showed me that merely storing knowledge does not preserve it over long periods. For old knowledge to have meaning, people have to relate it to their current problems and activities, translate it into contemporary language, and frame it within current issues. Thus, effective preserving looks much like applying. However, as social and technological changes accumulate, applying knowledge comes to look more like creating knowledge; and conversely, for newly created knowledge to have meaning, people must fit it into their current beliefs and perspectives.

* * *

In the mid-1980s, because I was teaching forecasting methods, I became interested in the accuracy of published forecasts (Barnett, Starbuck, and Pant 2003). A company called Predicast was reporting all of the forecasts they could find regarding US industries, and in another series of documents, they were also reporting outcome statistics that I could use to measure the accuracy of earlier forecasts. For four years, I employed various doctoral students to gather these data, specifying that I wanted only forecasts made between 1971 and 1977 that predicted events seven or more years into the future. Eventually, these students collected nearly 5,000 forecasts as well as outcome statistics matching roughly half of them. At that point, I graphed the data and found an interesting bimodal distribution that looked something like Figure 2.7. There appeared to be two superimposed distributions, the smaller one being composed of more optimistic forecasts; and forecasts about chemical industries comprised a high percentage of these optimistic forecasts. Thus, I conjectured that

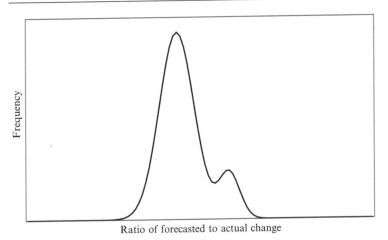

Figure 2.7 Ratio of forecasted change to actual change (original data)

chemical industries might have growth-oriented cultures that foster optimistic forecasts.

In 1993, Narayan Pant and I started to write an article based on the forecast data, but a few years had passed since the last student had added data, so we first went to the library to see if we could add more outcome statistics. We accidentally discovered some errors in the data recorded earlier, some of these errors minor but others significant. Indeed, we discovered quite a few errors. We decided that we should redo all of the data gathering. After weeks in the library, we had discarded roughly half of the earlier data but added nearly that many new observations. We now had 4,509 observations, 70 percent of which had matching outcome statistics, but half of these observations were entirely different from those in the original data and many other observations had had corrections. With these revised data, as Figure 2.8 shows, there was no longer a bimodal distribution.

My conjecture about chemical industries turned out to be a misperception arising from the fact that forecasts about chemical industries are very popular, so one can find numerous forecasts about chemical industries almost anywhere one looks. Yes, there is a small bulge to the right of the mode in Figure 2.8, but this bulge is not associated with a specific kind of industry. It is associated with a specific kind of forecasting. At a gross level, forecasts fall into four categories: some forecasts predict expected rates of change, some

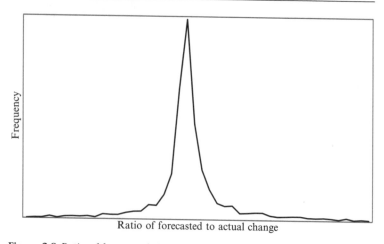

Ratio of forecasted to actual change

Figure 2.8 Ratio of forecasted change to actual change (revised data)

predict future quantities expressed in physical units such as tons or barrels, some predict monetary amounts in current dollars that incorporate expected price changes, and some predict monetary amounts in constant dollars that explicitly exclude price changes. Figure 2.9 gives the distributions of these four types, and as you can see, the optimistic forecasts are associated with forecasts about rates of change.

This experience revealed once again the risks of relying on other people to do work in which they have weak personal investments, it gave me a lesson in the ways search heuristics foster erroneous inferences, and it demonstrated that the error rates in some data can exceed 50 percent.

* * *

By the early 1990s, various earlier studies had reinforced each other to the point where I was conjecturing both that strategic planning does not help companies make higher profits and that much academic research uses very unreliable data (Starbuck 1985, 1992*b*). Firstly, there were the studies by Tosi, Aldag, and Storey (1973) and by Downey, Hellriegel, and Slocum (1975). These might have said that, on average, managers' perceptions of their environments' volatilities do not correlate with 'objective' measures of those volatilities. Secondly, there was Payne and Pugh's (1976) review of studies of how

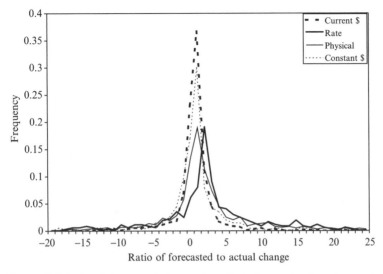

Figure 2.9 Ratio of forecasted change to actual change for four types of forecasts

people described their firms' structures and cultures. They had concluded that employees disagree greatly about their organizations' properties and that employees' perceptions of organizations' properties correlate weakly with 'objective' measures of those properties. Thirdly, there were the studies that Hedberg, Nystrom, and I had made of organizations facing serious crises. We had seen the top managers of firms developing views of their firms and their market environments that diverged greatly from what an outsider would have judged to be realistic. As well, in their study of twenty firms facing crises, Dunbar and Goldberg (1978) had found that many top managers surrounded themselves with yes-sayers, who filtered out signs of trouble and warnings from middle managers who tried to report problems. Fourthly, psychological studies of people's cognitions had revealed numerous biases and fantasies, some of which are very prevalent (Bazerman 1997). I thought that many managers probably exhibit such biases, and I also knew that many studies had pointed out how organizational documents attempt to mislead their readers by emphasizing financial and numerical data, by highlighting successes and rationalizing failures, and by giving senior executives credit for good results (Hofstede 1967; Hopwood 1972; Edelman

1977; Altheide and Johnson 1980; Dunbar 1981; Boland 1982; Bettman and Weitz 1983; Staw, McKechnie, and Puffer 1983).

Thus, I speculated that many managers, possibly most, might have erroneous perceptions of both their organizations and their business environments. As a result, I thought, most managers would be incapable of matching organizations to environments; and formal organizational analyses, carried out by groups of managers, would be very likely to yield incorrect results. Successful strategizing requires not only accurate perceptions of current organizational and environmental properties but also good forecasts of future developments. As a result, formal strategizing might be as likely to cause harm as to yield benefits.

Furthermore, these problems also cast doubt on many studies that relied on interviews with managers or on questionnaires completed by managers. If most managers do not actually know the properties of their organizations or their market environments, their answers to questions would have to express their beliefs rather than report 'objective facts'. Statistical analyses of such responses would reveal the beliefs that many managers share—what one might call managerial folklore. Although these shared beliefs would incorporate logical relations among concepts, these logical relations would be ones that accord with common sense and they might or might not accord with relations among 'objective' variables.

In 1993, John Mezias, a doctoral student, asked me to suggest some readings about managers' perceptions, especially studies assessing the accuracy of managers' perceptions. After reading the suggested studies, Mezias asked me why they had all appeared in the 1970s. Where were the recent studies? I proposed that he search for studies that were more recent. He searched several on-line databases but found no studies that compared managers' perceptions with 'objective' measures. We were both astonished at this null result. I urged Mezias to search again, but again he found nothing that assessed the accuracy of individual managers' perceptions. We then searched together and still did not find studies of the accuracy of managers' perceptions. Somewhat later, we learned that Sutcliffe (1994) had also searched for and found no such studies.

We thought that managers could not possibly be as far out of touch with their environments as implied by the old studies from the 1970s. Perhaps those old studies were misleading because they had not been designed to assess perceptual accuracy, and so their research methodology might have manufactured the observed perception errors. In particular, Tosi, Aldag, and Storey (1973) and Downey, Hellriegel, and Slocum (1975) had debated whether they should attribute the apparently very large errors in managers' answers to the managers or to their own research methods, and their 'objective' measures had been rather ad hoc. Therefore, we conjectured that a study designed specifically to assess perceptual accuracy would find much smaller perception errors, especially because we thought we could obtain better 'objective' measures.

We made two studies, the second better than the first (Starbuck and Mezias 1996; Mezias and Starbuck, 2003). To our disappointment, both studies showed that only about three-eighths of managers have rather accurate perceptions of their environments. Furthermore, we were unable to find patterns in the errors that would explain them or render them more predictable. In particular, partly because job titles are sometimes more symbolic than substantive, specialists did not have more accurate perceptions in their areas of specialization than nonspecialists did. Thus, our research brought me back to the skeptical position I had held in the late 1980s: Academic research that is based on managers' perceptions has a very unreliable foundation.

* * *

Our research into the errors in managers' perceptions coincidentally made me aware of another problem with spontaneous data. While investigating the reliability of 'objective' data that we could compare with what managers' said, we discovered the high error rates in widely available databases. In one audit, San Miguel (1977) found a 30 percent error rate in Compustat's reporting of R&D expenditures. These errors arose both from firms' reporting and from Compustat's processing. In a second audit, Rosenberg and Houghlet (1974) found much lower error rates in the stock prices reported by Compustat and by the Center for Research in Security Prices at the University of Chicago. About 2.4 percent of the stock prices contained errors but only 0.5 percent of the data had large enough errors to cause serious concern. Nevertheless, Rosenberg and Houghlet (1974: 1303) remarked, 'There are a few large errors in both databases, and these few errors are sufficient to change sharply the apparent nature of the data'. They advised researchers to compare data from different sources.

* * *

In 1993, Derek Pugh invited me to edit an anthology on premodern management thought, explaining that this meant writings from before 1880. I agreed to attempt this, not as an expert on premodern thought, but to learn something about it. A few weeks of reflection brought me to wondering about very ancient management practices—long before Niccolò Machiavelli or Robert Owen. I had seen descriptions of ancient practices only in a book by George (1968) that was so concise that it mainly roused my curiosity. Therefore, I asked the students in a doctoral seminar to investigate ancient management practices. Each student was to dig out evidence about actual management practices in one society. To keep the students from sliding too easily into well-known works and to push them toward serious library research, I told them to limit their search to times before the year 0 CE. Various students investigated ancient China, Greece, India, and Rome, and I investigated Egypt and Mesopotamia. In fact, the project continued for several years, as a couple of students and I dug more deeply into the surviving evidence (Rindova and Starbuck 1997*a*, 1997*b*).

The historical evidence again demonstrated the political character of spontaneous data. For example, Mesopotamia was home to several cultures and several languages through waves of migration and invasion, and the invasions often involved wholesale destruction of written records. More generally, works on papyrus, skins, or paper decayed unless scribes copied them, and scribes did so only if aristocrats approved of and valued the works. Copying introduced errors, and some scribes modernized works they were reproducing. The surviving texts represent only a small fraction of what once existed, and they are nonrandom samples. In one extreme case in 212 BCE, the first Chinese emperor burned nearly all the extant books and murdered nearly all the literate people. Wanting to replace the old feudal system with a new order, he sought to erase the traditions that had supported the old ways.

2.6 The 2000s

Writing a history of organization theory made me more conscious of the degree to which the twentieth century differed from earlier ones, and more conscious of the influence of MBA programs on academic research (Starbuck 2003*a*).

I speculate that generalizations about organizations resulted from social and technological changes during the last half of the nineteenth century and first half of the twentieth century. Changes in education, occupational and task specialization, and technologies caused a sudden increase in the numbers of large, formalized organizations, they made organizations relevant to many more people, and they made many more people interested in and capable of understanding abstract generalizations. Legal concepts also evolved and endowed corporations with 'personhood' that confers legal rights independent of the rights of their stakeholders. A distinct legal entity has to have definitive boundaries. Thus, both the similarity and distinctness of 'organizations' are social constructions that reflect large-scale social and technological changes.

This period also saw changes in the kinds of theories that people regarded as satisfying (Starbuck 2003*a*). Ancient tradition characterized societies as history-dependent organisms, analogous to the bodies of animals. This tradition held that social systems are not mere aggregates of individual people, for not only do individuals interact but also societies contain many interacting subsystems. Because events reflect both concepts about what should happen and external factors such as accidents and temporary conditions, explanations need to allow for the specifics of particular cases. Theories should describe the diversity of observed phenomena and fit them into evolutionary analytic frameworks. People are integrated creatures; human thinking occurs in human bodies; people have motives of which they are unconscious, and human actions are not always rational. Because people are not machines, it is both unrealistic and immoral to treat them as substitutable components in factories or bureaucracies.

However, organization theory took root in another, more 'modern' tradition that had risen to prominence during the seventeenth century and that regarded societies as machine-like. This mechanistic tradition saw the natural universe as a system of clockwork that follows timeless and immutable laws and sought theories that describe these causal laws. Abstract generalizations are better than concrete descriptions because they focus on durable essentials. Although the animal nature of humans corrupts their behavior, people should isolate and suppress their animalistic urges and strive to act solely on rational thought, which gives human reason a machine-like quality. Factories and bureaucracies achieve high productivity and reliability by training people to behave uniformly and consistently and treating them as substitutable components. By using their rationality, people can create stable and effective social systems.

Organization theory was also born of both perceived threats and perceived opportunities. From the 1860s to the 1960s, two themes dominated organization-theoretic writings. One theme asserted that bureaucracy has defects. Those who wrote about bureaucracy generally saw it as a vile threat to something—good government, control by rulers, individual freedom. Sociologists and economists paid much attention to how bureaucratic governments affect societies, and they expressed particular concern about bureaucracies' propensity to ignore their environments. However, some writers sought to describe bureaucracy's attractive qualities, so bureaucracy motivated organization theorists with both propulsion and repulsion. Because more admirers wrote earlier and more critics wrote later, the temporal trend formulated organization theory as the study of tribulations.

The second theme during the first half of the century was 'How can organizations operate more effectively?' Consultants and former managers discussed factories and other businesses, and they concentrated on identifying structural properties that influence organizations' productivity and responsiveness to top managers. They generally viewed organizations as offering attractive opportunities for something—efficient production, control by owners, cooperative effort. Most saw organizations as merely administrative hierarchies with well-defined tasks to perform, and they thought they were creating rigorous, scientific theories. Textbooks written during the very early years of the twentieth century talked about alternative ways to organize administrative hierarchies and to standardize procedures, but they devoted little attention to organizations as integrated systems. However, documents written during the 1920s began to view organizations as integrated systems and to discuss the structures of these systems. Later, Barnard (1937) and Simon (1944, 1950, 1952) saw organizations as offering opportunities to apply scientific research, especially social psychology.

The late 1940s and 1950s brought changes in the character of writings about organization theory. The sociological writings about bureaucracy and the managerial writings about organizational effectiveness discovered each other, and writings about organizations multiplied. Popular books and movies made the public aware of organizations' effects on employees (Wilson 1955; Whyte 1956).

Many sociologists published organizational studies; political scientists discussed intraorganizational power relations and decision-making in government; economists began to consider organizational factors; social psychologists discovered organizations as interesting settings for research.

By 1960, there were many more organization theorists and some had high social status. Organization theory had arrived, and the following decades offered organization theorists the beneficence of multiplying and expanding degree programs in business. Expansion and affluence brought pressures to fragment and to become self-absorbed and irrelevant to environmental problems.

Pressures for organization theory to become self-absorbed and irrelevant to its environment have come partly from its growing size and rising status and partly from the relevance of its subject matter for degree programs in business. Following 1950, collegiate business programs have provided steady and rapidly increasing funding. By 1956, nearly 43,000 Americans per year were graduating from collegiate business programs, and by 1998, this number had more than quintupled to 233,000 per year. In 1956, just over 3,000 Americans per year were graduating from MBA programs, and by 1998, this number had rocketed to more than 100,000 per year.

As organization theory grew larger and more respected, it also grew more autonomous from external constraints and more organized. Academics gained latitude to define what is interesting or important to themselves. Research methodology received ever more respect, and the most prevalent empiricism became a stylized type that isolates observers from those observed and allows observers to maintain detachment. Subtopics have proliferated and derived their popularity from their intellectual attractiveness. Organization theorists have created specialized divisions of professional associations and many specialized journals, including a few that have focused on subtopics within organization theory.

The themes that gave rise to organization theory have received little attention since 1960. Few organization theorists have focused on social problems associated with organizations. Although the old social problems still exist and new ones have appeared, researchers find it depressing to dwell on what is wrong and business students are not eager to discuss the sordid aspects of their future occupations. Few academic organization theorists have been seeking prescriptions for how organizations can become more productive, efficient, or effective. Prevalent management fads—such as Japanese management, downsizing, reengineering, teamwork, Quality Circles, Six-Sigma quality management, the Learning Organization, outsourcing, knowledge management—have been initiated by managers and consultants. Although some academic organization theorists have studied the consequences of such management fads, the most prestigious organization theorists have ignored them. The prestigious organization theorists have also generally ignored long-run changes in organizations' characteristics that have been stimulated by technological and population changes such as rising educational levels, computerization, telecommunication capacities, or globalization of firms.

Pressures to fragment have originated in the social sciences that organization theory spans. Whereas hostile environments can induce a collective enterprise to coalesce, multiple but friendly environments create ambivalence about participation in collective enterprise. One force toward fragmentation has come from the divide between psychology and sociology. A second force toward fragmentation has come from teachers and practitioners of 'strategic management', who sought legitimacy by defining a distinctive behavioral domain. A third force toward fragmentation has been dissatisfaction with the effectiveness of existing social theories, which has induced organization theorists to experiment with a wide range of diverse theories. Because it deals with complex phenomena, organization theory has drawn productively from very diverse intellectual domains, but newer ideas have supplemented older ideas rather than replaced them. A fourth force toward fragmentation has been culture, as theories and methodologies have evolved differently in different societies.

Organization theory has developed considerable complexity, so much complexity that doctoral students sometimes complain that it makes no sense to them. The students say that they do not understand how the fragments of organization theory relate to each other, how they differ, what each has to offer. Some of this apparent complexity is confusion created by researchers' efforts to trademark concepts, which have given multiple names to very similar concepts. More complexity has come from recognition of organizations' heterogeneity. Since organizations are diverse and complex, and since they inhabit diverse and complex environments, the complexity of organization theory makes sense. However, this complexity poses the classical dilemma of how complicated theories should be. Complex theories capture more aspects of what researchers observe, but they are hard to understand. Simple theories are easy to understand but they overlook phenomena that some people deem important.

* * *

In 2004, the editor of a prestigious journal wrote to one would-be author as follows:

Reviewer #2 points out that it would be very unusual for [this journal] to publish a paper that failed to find support for *any* of its hypotheses, as was the case in your paper. I think this is correct. When results fail to provide support for hypotheses, readers tend to look back at the theory that developed them and the research methods used to test them to find reasons for the disconfirming results. In many cases, this leads readers to find confirmation of suspicions raised when first encountering the theory and methods. I believe this was the case with your paper. I suspect that if you had found support for your hypotheses, the reviewers would have been more inclined to buy your theoretical ideas and [to] trust your methods. Because you did not, though, I suspect that the reviewers started to intensify their scrutiny of your theory and methods.

This editor's analysis of the psychology of reviewers strikes me as being correct, but it saddens me that methodology courses fail to teach researchers about the costs of such biases and that some journal editors tolerate or even reinforce them.

* * *

Also in 2004, the Attorney General of the State of New York filed a suit against GlaxoSmithKline alleging that the drug manufacturer had deceived consumers by publicizing the results of a trial that had produced evidence that a drug might offer significant benefits but had not publicized the results of four other trials that had produced evidence that this drug might have harmful effects or effects similar to placebos (Martinez 2004; Meier 2004*a*). According to Martinez (2004: B1), the New York Attorney General asserted that Glaxo's 'effort to suppress the other studies was harmful and improper to the doctors who were making prescribing decisions'. However, suppressing studies that have yielded insignificant findings is precisely what almost all academic journals do daily in the social sciences. Meier (2004a: C4) reported that a doctor who conducted a study that showed insignificant effects: 'wanted to report the study's findings...mainly because its negative results might have reflected trial design flaws that he did not want to see repeated in other studies. "I feel you need to present all the data even if it is negative", he said'. Two weeks after the suit was filed, Glaxo announced that they would henceforth report all clinical trials and their outcomes on their corporate website.

Around the time when New York filed its suit against Glaxo, the *American Journal of Psychiatry* published a study reporting that a clinical trial with an antidepressant drug had produced good results with children and teenagers (Meier 2004*b*). The trial had been sponsored by Forest Laboratories, the company that markets this drug in the USA, and the report's authors included three employees of Forest Laboratories. The published report of this trial did not mention a similar trial with the same drug, completed two years earlier in Denmark, that had found an insignificant difference between the drug and a placebo. The Danish trial had been sponsored by H. Lundbeck, the company that developed the drug, and a representative of H. Lundbeck stated that they had reported the trial results to Forest Laboratories. A representative for Forest Laboratories stated that the report of the new study had not cited the prior study because 'there was no citable public reference for the authors to examine', but Forest Laboratories had reported suicide-risk data from the Danish trial at a medical conference nine months earlier. According to Meier (2004*b*), 'Dr Nancy C. Andreasen, the editor of the *American Journal of Psychiatry*, which is the flagship publication of American Psychiatric Association, said it was the responsibility of a study's authors to provide a scholarly overview of the published articles discussed in their paper. She said that her publication did not specifically ask authors or companies that sponsor trials about unpublished studies'. Meier also reported:

[Editors of medical journals] say the challenges they face are not limited to the tendency by companies and academic researchers to showcase positive tests results while playing down trials with negative or inconclusive findings. Editors say they must also be vigilant against companies' cherry-picking favorable but limited data from a trial that had originally set out to test other aspects of a drug's performance—data mining. Some companies, several editors said, have also apparently milked tests for maximum publicity by submitting different parts of them under different authors' names to different medical journals.

Whittington et al. (2004: 1341) made a meta-analysis of clinical trials of Selective Serotonin reuptake inhibitors (SSRI) drugs for treating depression in children, including the trials mentioned above. They surmised:

Published data suggest a favourable risk-benefit profile for some SSRIs; however, addition of unpublished data indicates that risks could outweigh benefits of these drugs (except fluoxetine) to treat depression in children and young people. Clinical guideline development and clinical decisions about treatment are largely dependent on an evidence base published in peer-reviewed journals. Non publication of trials, for whatever reason, or the omission of important data from published trials, can lead to erroneous recommendations for treatment. Greater openness and transparency with respect to all intervention studies is needed.

Parallels to social science research and to publications in social science journals seem clear, except that the public and the government have shown stronger interest in having unbiased information about medical research.

3

Pretences of Research

We have met the enemy and he is us.

—Pogo (Walt Kelly) 1970

This chapter surveys the problems that I see as major ones for social science research. The overall theme linking these problems is that researchers do what serves them personally in preference to what promotes the creation of reliable knowledge. Because researchers disagree about the existence and nature of knowledge and because research practices preserve the uncertainty of what is known, there is never closure, and never an end to ambiguity. Because researchers focus on producing articles rather than knowledge and because all researchers are able to claim to have made discoveries, there are no limits to researchers' potential productivity and no serious challenges to their genius. Because contributions to knowledge reflect the characteristics of human bodies and social systems, research typically reveals more about the researchers themselves and their assumptions than about the topics they study. The general effect is to make research a pretence rather than a source of genuine contributions to knowledge.

3.1 What Does Science Have to Do with Knowledge?

Merely mentioning 'knowledge' raises problems, for anyone with the temerity to write about knowledge has to confront pervasive disagreement about what constitutes knowledge. When I was investigating knowledge-intensive firms in the early 1990s, I organized a faculty seminar on knowledge management. Well over a dozen professors said they would like to attend and to speak about their research on knowledge. The successive speakers adopted diverse viewpoints, discussed diverse issues, and proposed diverse applications. So varied were the contributions that one could say that the speakers agreed on only one point: none of them agreed with the others about the proper definition of knowledge. Indeed, every speaker began by explaining his or her distinctive definition of knowledge.

Thus, I have no illusions that I can offer views about knowledge that everyone will accept. However, I believe that scientific research has the primary purpose of creating knowledge that is objectively true, so I need to explain what I mean by these words (Calhoun and Starbuck 2003). What is knowledge and what makes it 'objective truth'?

Webster's Third International Dictionary offers eight definitions for knowledge, but all are variations on two themes: (*a*) thorough familiarity; and (*b*) perception of facts or truth. The second of these themes is more relevant for researchers. Although some teachers see themselves as trying to produce thorough familiarity in students, few researchers see themselves as trying to produce thorough familiarity. Rather, insofar as researchers see themselves as creators of knowledge, they see themselves as trying to produce knowledge that other people accept as fact or truth.

Acceptance by other people is crucial, for knowledge is what people say it is. People, individually and collectively, decide what they regard as knowledge, so human physiology and human social systems mold human understanding of facts or truths and they influence definitions of knowledge. Even people who believe in the existence of absolute truths have to observe them through human perceptual systems. Indeed, Polanyi (1962) argued that because observations always reflect the humans who make them, science can never be completely objective.

Social systems are also crucial because social processes elevate perceptions into facts, convert beliefs into truths. I find useful Brunsson's (1982) notion of a continuum between subjectivity and objectivity. At one extreme, a perception or belief held by only one person has the status of being subjective, and it directly affects the actions by that person only. At the other extreme, a widely shared perception or belief acquires the status of being objective, not only can it affect the actions of many people but these people also see their actions as having the support of objective fact. Indeed, to motivate large-scale collective action, a perception or belief must be widely shared. When a perception or belief gains consensus support, it acquires the status of truth. Of course, no perception or belief has the support of total consensus, and in that respect, no perception or belief constitutes total truth, but communication, social influence, and consensus building certainly play central roles in defining knowledge.

Science has a respected status in human affairs because people generally perceive science to be capable of producing knowledge on which almost everyone is willing to rely. This willingness arises from a shared conviction that scientific principles offer highly effective guidance for how researchers can generate knowledge. Students learn to respect these principles in school, where they hear that scientific principles produce reliable knowledge and that rational thought is an effective tool for analyzing situations and for creating or selecting actions. In addition, belief in the effectiveness of scientific principles and in the willingness and ability of researchers to follow these principles is very important to the integration of modern societies. People use scientific findings to resolve disagreements between dearly held ethical or political positions, to resolve uncertainties in legal cases, to assign responsibility for errors and achievements, to assess the costs and benefits accruing from social policies, and so forth. Of course, for research to perform such functions, it has to engender confidence in its reliability, and this requires that research express the spirit of scientific principles, not observe them merely symbolically.

This chapter argues that social science research falls short of its potential by engaging in activities that do not engender confidence in its reliability. Some of these practices block the accumulation of knowledge, some erect facades of scientific rigor around meaningless activities, and some fail to allow for the limitations of human abilities.

3.2 Never-Ending Ambiguity

For research to create knowledge, not only must researchers agree among each other that some beliefs and perceptions are correct but also such agreements have to be nearly universal. When researchers continue to repeat questions, either no one has developed satisfactory answers for those questions or social processes have not established consensuses that current answers are satisfactory.

There are certainly beliefs on which researchers agree, and some of these have nearly universal agreement. Kuhn (1962) argued that consensus among researchers creates stable research paradigms. These paradigms, he said, define criteria for choosing problems and issues as well as methodologies, and knowledge develops for rather long periods within the specifications of a paradigm. Paradigms tend to have long lives because, when consensus exists about an existing paradigm, a novel theory or methodology runs into stiff opposition.

Consensus favoring use of null-hypothesis significance tests affords a clear example of paradigm stability. Although methodologists have been trying to discourage the use of these tests since the 1950s, the tests have remained very prevalent, and there is no sign that social scientists are shifting to other criteria. Hubbard and Ryan (2000) measured the use of such tests by psychological researchers. Figure 3.1 shows their basic finding, which is that nearly all psychological articles use these tests. Hubbard and Ryan (2000: 678) concluded: 'It seems inconceivable to admit that a methodology as bereft of value as SST (statistical significance tests) has survived, as the centerpiece of inductive inference no less, more than four decades of criticism in the psychology literature.'

Fidler et al. (2004) examined what happened after some editors attempted to ban or to reduce the use of significance tests. Researchers

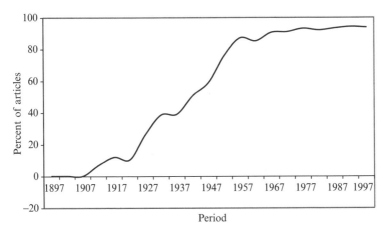

Figure 3.1 Frequency of significance tests in twelve psychological journals
(Adapted from Hubbard and Ryan 2000)

had complied with the journals' restrictions only in the tables that presented results of calculations, and the researchers had continued to speak of significance levels in their verbal interpretations of results. Thus, the notions of statistical significance are so ingrained that most researchers find it impossible not to rely on them when interpreting their findings.

Researchers' consensus support of null-hypothesis significance tests contrasts sharply with researchers' disagreements about the substantive findings from research. In many fields, and certainly in the social and economic sciences, researchers act as if they doubt the validity of prior research. Reviews of prior research highlight the ambiguity and inconsistency of findings, and researchers routinely dismiss prior findings and propose new propositions. Social scientists treat minor variations on existing theories as if they were major achievements, including distinctive new names. Indeed, consensuses in the social and economic sciences mainly endorse tautological theories or research practices that preserve the uncertainty of findings. As a result, there is never closure and ambiguity always persists.

Many social science contributions have to be incremental or less because old knowledge deteriorates unless someone restates it in terms of contemporary concepts and issues. Thus, social scientists cannot merely build on previous achievements; they must rephrase those achievements. For instance, ancient Chinese literature includes a document that foreshadowed modern contingency theories of leadership (Rindova and Starbuck 1997a). 'The Great Plan' mentions 1121 BCE but includes passages older than 2200 BCE. Its passage about leadership has two interpretations. One interpretation focuses on different types of subordinates, and advises leaders to consider two dimensions of their followers—their attitudes toward social order and their attitudes toward work:

The three virtues are rules, firmness, and gentleness. Spell out rules for peaceful people; deal firmly with violent and offensive people; deal gently with amenable and friendly people. Employ firm supervision with those who shirk or lack initiative, gentle supervision with those who are distinguished by their talents and good dispositions. (Karlgren 1950, 1970)

These statements resemble the modern Vertical Dyad Linkage theory about how leaders actually do behave. Liden and Graen (1980) said leaders reward subordinates who show commitment and who expend a lot of effort by showing them consideration, trusting them and giving them information. Toward other subordinates, leaders act impersonally and rigidly.

The second interpretation of 'The Great Plan' focuses on different situations, and advises supervisors to consider two kinds of contingencies—the social context and the people they are supervising:

The three virtues are correct procedure, strong management, and mild management. Adhere to correct procedure in situations (times) of peace and tranquility; use strong management in situations of violence and disorder; apply mild management in situations of harmony and order. Employ strong supervision with people who lack initiative, mild supervision with the honorable and intelligent. (Legge 1865; Chan 1963; Karlgren 1970)

These statements resemble Fiedler's modern contingency theory about how leaders ought to behave (Fiedler 1967). Fiedler argued that leadership styles should match 'situational favorableness', which takes account of leader–member relationship, degree of task structure, and a leader's formal authority. Table 3.1 compares 'The Great Plan's' situational interpretation with Fiedler's theory. Fiedler's task-directed and human relations–directed styles are not very different from the strong and mild styles in 'The Great Plan'. Fiedler's very unfavorable situations resemble situations of violence and disorder because these are times of low trust in leaders, low authority and power of leaders, and changing tasks. Fiedler's very favorable situations resemble situations of peace and tranquility because the opposite conditions hold. Fiedler's moderately favorable situations resemble situations of harmony and order because controlled moderate change does not disrupt political leadership.

Table 3.1 Two theories of leadership: 'The Great Plan' versus Fiedler

Situation	'The Great Plan's' advice	Fiedler's advice
Very unfavorable Violence and disorder	Strong	Task-directed
Moderately favorable Harmony and order	Mild	Human relations–directed
Very favorable Peace and tranquility	Correct procedure	Task-directed

Thus, when Fiedler or Liden and Graen receive credit for having invented their theories, they are receiving credit for restating some very old ideas in modern language. Modern managers would not find the prescriptions in 'The Great Plan' persuasive even if they understood the words because they would wonder how well research has supported the prescriptions, and they might ask for examples of how the prescriptions relate to situations in the contemporary world. By presenting statistical evidence and citing corroborative research, Fiedler and Liden and Graen conferred authenticity to their ideas, at least to academics, and by giving modern examples of the ideas in use, they demonstrated how to apply them.

Social science empiricism rarely produces clear answers. To run controlled experiments, researchers generally have to study very artificial situations, with the result that experimental findings probably do not extrapolate to realistic situations. For instance, researchers cannot persuade large numbers of experienced business executives to participate in experiments, and researchers cannot offer the large financial incentives that are present in real business situations, so they enlist undergraduate students to pretend implausibly that they are business executives making decisions that have very small financial consequences. Experiments with real social systems lack controls and occur mutatis mutandis, so findings are very difficult to interpret. As a result, researchers try to infer general principles from observations of specific instances. All data describe specific instances, which are potentially deceptive, always somewhat unique, and often context driven. Since records and surveys always contain biases and errors, data from such sources inherit their defects. Self-reporting problems and the use of proxies render most data inaccurate and the links between data and theories tenuous. Researchers frame their projects in terms of concepts and language that seem irrelevant or meaningless to people in real-world contexts, which makes it difficult for researchers to communicate with their subjects (Cappelli and Sherer 1991; Starbuck and Mezias 1996). Data often violate the assumptions made in analyses, rendering the analyses speculative and misleading. Because researchers are normally aware that several hypotheses are consistent with their data or that missing data could alter their inferences, almost all empirical studies call, implicitly or explicitly, for better studies. Moreover, when researchers evaluate each other's studies, they usually disagree about the value of the work.

Indeed, researchers' evaluations of findings in the social sciences imply that the evaluators feel a need to look beyond findings and methodology per se in order to evaluate research. For example, Mahoney (1977, 1979) submitted five manuscripts to seventy-five people who had recently reviewed for the *Journal of Applied Behavior Analysis*. The manuscripts were nearly identical except that some of them reported negative results, some positive results, and some mixed results. Mahoney chose reviewers whose publications implied that they were likely to prefer positive results, and indeed, reviewers did generally award higher ratings for scientific contribution to the manuscripts that reported positive results and reviewers were much more likely to recommend acceptance or minor revision of manuscripts that reported positive results. The interrater correlations were low, however, even though all reviewers shared similar biases toward positive results. The interrater correlations were 0.30 for recommendations about publication and ratings of scientific contribution, and close to zero for ratings of methodology, relevance, and the quality of discussion. Yet, ratings of methodology correlated a very high 0.94 with recommendations about publication. It appears that reviewers criticize the methodology of studies they would not like to see in print, which tend to be ones contradicting the theories they prefer; and they applaud the methodology of studies they would like to see in print, which tend to be ones that are supporting the theories they prefer.

Other studies have also reported reviewers' biases. Mahoney, Kazdin, and Kenigsberg (1978) found that reviewers are more likely to render favorable opinions about manuscripts that cite in-press studies by the manuscripts' authors. Nylenna, Riis, and Karlsson (1994) observed that Scandinavian reviewers give higher ratings to manuscripts written in English than to the same manuscripts written in the authors' native Scandinavian languages. Horrobin (1990) is one of several authors who have complained that reviewers with investments in prior research impede the publication of innovative research, with one result being that more innovative research tends to appear in lower-status journals. Ellison (2002) found that review processes of economics journals take longer when manuscripts fall into editors' areas of specialization, possibly because the editors do more nitpicking.

Perhaps the most discussed and controversial study of peer review was the one by Peters and Ceci (1982), who resubmitted twelve articles to the journals that had published them just 18–32 months earlier. All twelve journals were highly regarded ones, and the articles had originally been written by authors from prestigious psychology departments. However, the resubmissions bore fictitious authors' names and return addresses at obscure institutions. The submissions went to thirty-eight editors and reviewers. Three of these editors or reviewers detected that the articles had already been published, which cut the sample to nine articles that had eighteen reviewers. Sixteen of the eighteen reviewers recommended rejection, and the editors rejected eight of the nine articles. The most prevalent reasons for rejection were 'serious methodological flaws', including inappropriate statistical analyses and faulty study design.

Two kinds of observations offer tangential evidence about the reliability of reviewers' judgments. Firstly, Gottfredson (1977, 1978) found that reviewers' forecasts of manuscripts' impacts correlated only 0.37 with later citations and their ratings of manuscripts' quality correlated only 0.24 with later citations. Secondly, Table 3.2 shows confidence limits for the reported correlations between reviewers' judgments for all the studies of social science journals I have found. The correlations range from near zero to over 0.5 (Starbuck 2003*b*, 2005).

Although a few authors and editors have speculated that interrater agreement tends to be higher where journals have narrower foci, the evidence for this notion is weak. It is unclear whether there is more agreement among reviewers for more specialized journals. Although more homogeneous reviewers should tend to agree with each other, more homogeneous manuscripts give emphasis to smaller differences among reviewers. Gottfredson (1978), Gottfredson and Gottfredson (1982), and Wolff (1970) have reported that reviewers for psychological journals agree strongly about the properties they want manuscripts to exhibit, but they agree much less strongly about whether specific manuscripts exhibit these properties. The correlations between reviewers range from 0.16 to 0.50 when the reviewers evaluate the properties of specific manuscripts. Gottfredson (1977, 1978) found that reviewers make distinctions between the quality of a manuscript and its probable impact on its field, but reviewers' ratings of impact correlate only 0.14 with later citations of the published articles. In fact, the practical correlation is nil because reviewers' ratings of impact correlate 0.03 with later citations for most articles. The average correlation is higher across all articles because a few

Table 3.2 Observed correlations between two reviewers (Starbuck 2005)

Journal	95% confidence limits for correlation between reviewers	
	Below	Above
Journal of Abnormal Psychology, 1976 (Cicchetti and Eron 1979)	−0.02	0.18
Journal of Abnormal Psychology, 1975 (Cicchetti and Eron 1979)	0.04	0.26
Administrative Science Quarterly (Starbuck 2003)	0.05	0.19
Journal of Abnormal Psychology, 1973 (Cicchetti and Eron 1979)	0.06	0.26
Sociometry (Hendrick 1976, 1977)	0.08	0.34
Developmental Review (Whitehurst 1984)	0.09	0.45
Journal of Abnormal Psychology, 1977 (Cicchetti and Eron 1979)	0.10	0.30
Personality and Social Psychology Bulletin (Hendrick 1976, 1977)	0.11	0.33
Journal of Personality and Social Psychology (Scott 1974)	0.16	0.36
Journal of Abnormal Psychology, 1974 (Cicchetti and Eron 1979)	0.19	0.41
American Sociological Review (Hargens and Herting 1990; Cicchetti 1991)	0.20	0.38
American Psychologist (Cicchetti 1991)	0.20	0.56
Journal of Educational Psychology (Marsh and Ball 1981)	0.25	0.43
Social Problems (Smigel and Ross 1970)	0.38	0.59
American Psychologist (Cicchetti 1991)	0.38	0.70
American Psychologist (Scarr and Weber 1978; Cicchetti 1980)	0.49	0.76

articles receive high impact ratings from reviewers and also many later citations.

After much analysis, considering various contingencies, my inference is that the correlation of a single reviewer's judgment with the actual quality of a reviewed manuscript normally falls between 0.25 and 0.3, and this correlation does not often fall below 0.05 or range above 0.37 (Starbuck 2005). These correlations say quite a lot about the quality differences among journals. Because reviewers are likely to make erroneous judgments, highly prestigious journals publish some low-value articles and low-prestige journals publish some excellent articles. When reviewers' judgments correlate around 0.3 with manuscripts' quality, over half of the articles published are not among the best manuscripts that were submitted to those journals. When reviewers' judgments correlate around 0.15 with manuscripts' quality, over three-quarters of the articles published are not among the best manuscripts that were submitted to those journals (Starbuck 2005). Rousseeuw (1991: 41) described the situation humorously, saying, 'It is commonly known and a constant course of frustration that even well-known refereed journals contain a large fraction of bad articles which are boring, repetitive, incorrect, redundant, and harmful to science in general. What is perhaps even worse, the same journals also stubbornly reject some brilliant and insightful articles (i.e. your own) for no good reason.' He then argued that because 'bad papers are submitted in such vast quantities... the small fraction of them that gets accepted may outnumber the good ones' (Rousseeuw 1991: 43).

3.3 Unlimited Productivity

Since research is an occupation that involves prestige and salaries, one should expect to see career-oriented behavior, and one does. Social scientists seem to be more concerned with producing papers than with producing knowledge. It is one conceit of this age that knowledge can be mass-produced—indeed, that researchers can be mass-produced. If there is something we do not know, we need only to spend more money and train more researchers. As a result, research methods that lend themselves to mass-production—the archetype being statistical analyses of databases that were created through mail surveys—are prevalent. If consumers of research accept mass-produced findings as contributions to knowledge, researchers have weak incentive to undertake projects that are more challenging.

Closely linked to mass-production is democratization. The underlying notion is that since researchers can be mass-produced, anyone who has basic research credentials is equally capable of judging the value of proposed research or reports of completed research. A senior official in the US government once explained to me that the nation could cut the cost of producing Ph.Ds in half by funding their education at the University of Kentucky instead of Harvard University. Agencies that fund research systematically recruit young reviewers as well as older ones, reviewers from obscure universities as well as from prestigious ones, and reviewers from diverse ethnic groups. The editors of journals rarely tell authors that they should pay more attention to the comments of some reviewers than others, and the employees of funding agencies are not supposed to assign more credibility to some reviewers than others. Hence, the research grants tend to go to projects that look most conventional and have the broadest audiences, and research that conforms to mass-production norms is more likely to receive favorable editorial review.

It is another conceit of this age that achievements can be measured numerically. Various periodicals rank universities and departments, which respond by trying to achieve on the measures that go into the rankings. The Institute for Scientific Information compiles statistics that feed rankings of journals' 'impacts'. Universities and departments urge professors to do things that will help them achieve higher rankings, meaning more articles in journals with higher rankings or articles that receive more citations. Stripped to its economic foundation, higher education is a highly competitive industry with very large amounts of money at stake and with very short-term goals, such as high scores on various rating scales, large numbers of applicants, and large contributions from donors.

Thus, both researchers and their employers appreciate a system that places no limits on the production of knowledge. Every university wants to be able to point to geniuses in its faculty, people who have made important discoveries, possibly many of them. My next-door neighbor once told me admiringly that one of his colleagues, a chemist who specialized in Boron, had completed forty papers during a one-month vacation in the mountains. Widespread belief at his university held that this chemist was virtually certain to receive the Nobel Prize one day, which he in fact did fifteen years later. Researchers want to be sure that they can continue to succeed and possibly to move upward in their occupations, so they cherish routines that assure them of their productivity and criteria for success that emphasize extreme effort and conformity to social norms. Doctoral students want to believe that the research methods they are studying really do work, that the topics discussed in journals really do matter, and that they can gain successful careers by following the examples of their teachers. Incremental contributions, even noncontributions, have high value because researchers have investments in existing methods and theories. Researchers are all too aware that their high statuses depend on their mastery of relevant knowledge, meaning the knowledge already at hand, and radically new knowledge could render them obsolete and displace them from control (Normann 1971; Starbuck 1983*b*).

When people see their statements and actions as influencing their career success and long-term economic welfare, they try to make their statements and actions defensible. Faust (1978) explained that researchers face a challenge of positioning proposed research to attract investment and funding. Researchers cannot be sure of producing favorable outcomes because outcomes are not always favorable and evaluations are unreliable, so they highlight the correctness of their analyses and the thoroughness of their literature reviews. Just as decision makers try to demonstrate that they had good plans whether or not the plans were achieved, researchers try to show that they used good methods whether or not those methods produced scientific progress. These effects grow stronger when researchers attach their names to theories.

Admittedly, even trivial research serves social functions for both researchers and their audiences. Continuing to strive enables people to believe that they can comprehend someday. Continuing to 'create knowledge' gives people feelings of self-efficacy, self-confidence, and hope for future improvements. Consider, for instance, the innumerable articles in newspapers and magazines that describe recent 'advances' in medical research and speculate about future treatments. Periodicals publish so many of these articles because their readers want to read about progress and the promise of a better future.

However, too much effort goes into generating meaningless research 'findings' and the flood of meaningless 'contributions' probably obscures some discoveries that would really be useful. Using null-hypothesis significance tests to judge hypotheses important is a major source of this flood. In industrial psychology, two-thirds of the reported correlations are statistically significant at the 5-percent level (Webster and Starbuck 1988). Starting with a randomly chosen target variable and drawing a second variable at random from the population of social science studies, a researcher would need only three trials to find a variable that correlates significantly with the target variable. As a result, significance tests are highlighting multitude correlations that have no theoretical meaning. Meaningful relations are being lost in clouds of random errors, and virtually no hypothesis is ever ruled out definitively.

Another source of meaningless 'contributions' is the use of ordinary least-squares regression with small samples. Because squared errors give extreme weight to low-probability observations, regression calculations are less reliable than the researchers' a priori assumptions unless samples sizes are large. Studies have shown that one needs 200–400 observations even when the data have perfect Normal distributions (Schmidt, 1971; Claudy 1972; Einhorn and Hogarth 1975); and when data depart from Normality, one might need several thousand observations (Starbuck and Mezias 1996). Yet, social scientists routinely publish least-squares regressions with samples smaller than 200. Such ritualistic research methods resemble the croquet game in Wonderland: The Queen of Hearts, said Alice, 'is so extremely likely to win that it is hardly worthwhile finishing the game.' If a theory can win only a ritualistic competition, it would be better to leave the theory unpublished.

Social science research also has limitless boundaries because many researchers strive to create generally valid theories. In the interests of generality, each study suggests the possibility of additional studies of slightly different situations. However, this pursuit of generality ultimately undermines the value of the theories. As researchers modify their measures to encompass more diverse situations, the measures emphasize more commonplace phenomena (Starbuck 1981).

When researchers truly believe their theories, they find correction factors that eliminate the theories' value, for a theory that is true everywhere has to be tautological. One oft-cited example is microeconomic theory, which its users regard as axiomatic and others see as vacuous. Because its users insist that this theory cannot be incorrect, they revise their analyses retrospectively, but retrospective interpretations can neither be disproved nor confirmed. A less well-known example is afforded by the macroeconomic analysis that brought Robert Solow the Nobel Prize in Economic Sciences. Seeking to describe the relation among labor, capital, and output, Solow (1957) introduced technology as the missing ingredient. He then estimated the effects of technology by calculating the amounts of technological change that would have created an almost perfect relationship among labor, capital, and output. He assumed that this relationship might take one of five algebraic forms, and Table 3.3 shows the multiple correlations he obtained with each of these forms. Obviously, the fits

Table 3.3 Correlations in Solow's analysis of the aggregate production function

Model (hypothesized algebraic function)	Multiple correlation
$\Delta q = \alpha + \beta k$	0.9982
$q = \alpha + \beta \log k$	0.9996
$q = \alpha - \beta/k$	0.9964
$\log q = \alpha + \beta \log k$	0.9996
$\log q = \alpha - \beta/k$	0.9980

were very close with every algebraic form, which he interpreted as evidence for the validity of his theory. But Table 3.3 suggests that the method of calculation eliminated nearly all the differences between algebraic forms, and indeed, the only reason the multiple correlations were not all exactly 1.00 is that Solow used a first-order approximation when he calculated the effects of technology. As a result, the high correlations in Table 3.3 give no information about the correspondence between Solow's theory and his data. His method of calculating the effects of technology would have produced arbitrarily tight fits to any data whatever.

However, changing from less productive research methods to more productive ones would not decimate career opportunities, for social science research pursues ever-advancing goals. Firstly, although most research is supposed to help people to understand the present and future, all researchers study the past and all data come from the past, sometimes the distant past. Even data about what was happening at the time of data gathering are no longer current by the time someone has analyzed them. People and social systems change constantly, and from time to time, they change dramatically. Changes call for additional studies that examine the altered situations. Dramatic examples of this phenomenon occurred with the design of highway systems for major metropolitan areas. In some cities, the designers started by surveying drivers' sources and destinations and then analyzed these survey data to develop routes that would benefit the most drivers. Then it took from five to twenty years to build the actual highways, by which time the original data had grown obsolete; factories had moved, neighborhoods had changed, new suburbs had sprung up, shopping centers had appeared. Other cities made no efforts to study travel patterns and merely built highways where land was available. In the end, it turned out that the carefully planned highways worked no better than did highways that other cities had located without regard for current travel patterns (Starbuck 1983a).

Secondly, insofar as researchers do acquire knowledge, they or other people often use this knowledge to add more complexity to technological or social systems, with one result being that people become ignorant once again. Bridge building offers an example. People have been building bridges for many, many millennia. Yet bridges collapse almost every year, often because new knowledge has induced bridge builders to go outside the envelope of experience and to experiment with novel designs. The Challenger disaster presents another example (Starbuck and Milliken 1988). As soon as NASA thought they had a space vehicle that worked well, they began to introduce modifications to enable the vehicle to carry heavier payloads. To save weight, they made the metal skin of the rocket engine slightly thinner; they shifted to a slightly more powerful rocket fuel; and they made the nozzle of the rocket engine slightly smaller. Each of these modifications was only a small increment to one feature, but each took the system slightly outside the envelope of experience, and three such modifications interacted to produce amplified effects. The smaller nozzle and more powerful fuel increased the pressure inside the rockets, as they were supposed to do, and the thinner skin flexed more when subjected to pressure. As a result, the joints between sections of the rocket began to leak flame and hot gases, which ultimately caused disaster.

3.4 Comfortable Knowledge

As a product of human activity, a product created for human consumption, research has to reflect the characteristics of people, either as individuals or as collectivities. In particular, researchers do what they know how to do and what makes them comfortable. Yet familiar, comfortable methodologies may be ineffective, and researchers may be blind to the limitations of their methodologies and the limitations of their own abilities. While acknowledging that many scientific failures result from inadequate data, subjective biases, and inappropriate questions, Faust (1984: 116) remarked that the most fundamental problem may be humans' insufficient cognitive ability: 'Scientists may have sufficient cognitive ability to comprehend simple configural relationships among cues or variables, but insufficient ability to comprehend more complex relationships.'

Human rationality confers significant disadvantages. It seeks to classify almost everything into bifurcated categories, and in so doing, it erases fine distinctions and converts faint relations into close ones. It warps humans' observations (Singer and Benassi 1981). People see phenomena that their logic tells them they ought to see even when the phenomena do not actually occur. People remember events that never took place (Kiesler 1971; Nisbett and Wilson 1977; Loftus 1979). Circumstances and environmental influences can dramatically influence human perception and information processing. Consider victims of severe abuse who begin to identify with their captors or abusers. Or, consider the views expressed by cults and religious or political factions. Human rationality can extrapolate incomplete knowledge to impossible extremes (Starbuck 1988).

Rationality arises from human physiology; our minds feel comfortable when we perceive relations as being logical, and our shared rationality helps us to understand what others are saying. Because it arises from human physiology, rationality is something that everyone can recognize in an argument and agree that it is good. However, we have no guarantee that rational logic is adequate to the tasks we assign to it. The Law of Requisite Variety says that for people to understand their environments, human comprehension abilities must be as complex and diverse as the environments (Ashby 1961). But, human rationality is a rather crude and imperfect tool, with very limited powers of discrimination, so humans' environments may be more complex than people are able to grasp. Hayek (1975: 92) observed: 'It may indeed prove to be far the most difficult and not the least important task for human reason rationally to comprehend its own limitations.'

The philosophy guiding scientific research relies very strongly on the correctness of rationality. Indeed, scientific rationality is an extreme ideal type that has been constructed through centuries of discussion by philosophers and scientists, and implanted in researchers through education and socialization. One can observe participants in academic seminars shifting into a ritualistic mode of rationality. This mode reduces all conditions to binary states—good or evil, true or false, consistent or inconsistent. It rejects loose ends and fosters ludicrous extrapolations. It generates logical contradictions when we oversimplify complexities; it distorts our observations as we refuse to see what is illogical and insist on seeing what we expect; and it converts incomplete knowledge into absurd implications. We seek scientific rationality because it gives our minds satisfaction, but what puts our minds at ease may not give us insight or useful knowledge.

Of course, much of the time, researchers do not actually follow the prescriptions for rational thought that are supposed to guide scientific research. These deviations have both beneficial and harmful consequences. The deviations are beneficial insofar as they prevent people from carrying rationality to ridiculous extremes (Starbuck 1983b). Bazerman (1997) documented more than a dozen heuristics and biases that shape human thought. For instance, people tend to see themselves as causing events and they underestimate the effects of external causes. People especially emphasize their own impacts after they succeed, and they emphasize the effects of environmental causes after other people succeed. In public forums such as research seminars, social statuses influence rationality, as there is a general presumption that more prestigious participants present the most rational and relevant arguments.

The limitations of human mental capacities require that human knowledge be simplistic. Even researchers who advocate multivariate analyses fall back upon bivariate and trivariate interpretations when they try to explain what their analyses really mean. When Box and Draper (1969) attempted to use experiments to discover more effective ways to operate factories, they concluded that practical experiments should manipulate only two or three variables at a time because the people who interpret the experimental findings have too much difficulty making sense of interactions among four or more variables. Faust (1984) pointed out the difficulties that scientists have in understanding four-way interactions (Meehl, 1954; Goldberg 1970); he noted that the great theoretical contributions to the physical sciences have exhibited parsimony and simplicity rather than complexity.

Possibly, more problematic than the limitations of human physiology are the limitations created by human collectivities. It is the organizations that employ researchers that are stressing quantitative measures of research output and pressing researchers to generate more of less. As employers who control the wages and social statuses of their employees, employing organizations can powerfully influence researchers' behavior. As competitors for students, wealth, and social status, employing organizations pursue goals that are inconsistent with what is needed to make research effective.

Professional collectivities corrupt research efforts by defining methods ritualistically and by protecting vested interests. One example of dysfunctional professional norms, pointed out in the preceding chapter, is the tolerance of misleading language to exaggerate the generality and importance of research findings. Researchers use definite articles to describe representative instances—the organization, the firm, the manager—in situations where indefinite articles would be accurate. Professional norms also allow researchers to describe their observations broadly without specifying the degrees to which their statements are valid. For instance, a researcher who has found that the average height of men exceeds the average height of women is permitted to say 'men are taller than women'. These exaggerations often occur as interpretations of statistical significance tests. Indeed, the very labels 'significance' and 'significant' exaggerate the importance of research findings. Another example of dysfunctional professional norms is the tolerance, and sometimes advocacy, of retrospective analyses of spontaneous data. Researchers overlook the many biases in spontaneous data because these are available and cheap, and retrospective analyses assure researchers of success because they know what their theories must explain. A third example of dysfunctional professional norms is the primacy of 'methodological rigor'. Since no study is ever as rigorous as it could have been, those who dislike specific findings can rationalize them or protest their publication on methodological grounds. A study attracts respect if its author uses an esoteric methodology with an impressive name, and no researcher has a strong defense against an accusation of inadequate methodology. Of course, such professional norms generally have strong support from researchers who have been 'successful'. The norms allow researchers to have predictable, fairly stable careers, and they work to the advantage of researchers who are more willing to conform to social norms, who tend to be 'leaders' in their professions.

3.5 How Well Does It Work?

Although people honor scientific methods and credit them with multitude achievements, the effectiveness of scientific methods is a hypothesis that must be tested in practice. The validity of this hypothesis depends on how people concretize scientific methods, and as practiced, scientific methods seem to be considerably less effective than they could be. The evidence suggests that scientific methods are generally not very effective in creating useful knowledge or enhancing our abilities to produce desired outcomes.

Although research methodologies vary among fields, all scientific fields endorse a few core principles: (*a*) Researchers should make the creation of knowledge an overriding goal that supersedes all other goals, including political and religious ones. (*b*) Researchers should not only be honest and truthful but also should tell the whole truth, including their doubts about their findings. (*c*) Researchers should build on the work of their predecessors, so that knowledge accumulates over time. (*d*) Results should be clear enough to speak for themselves.

However, the evidence suggests that much social science research does not adhere to these principles, and there is some evidence that much research about human behavior fails to produce any knowledge whatever. In particular, social science fields devote efforts to generating numerous additional hypotheses without excluding any current hypotheses, many journals regularly refuse to print studies that fail to reject null hypotheses, and many published articles reject null hypotheses that are probably true (Greenwald 1975; Blaug 1980). Even worse, editors and reviewers regularly urge authors to misrepresent their actual research processes by inventing 'hypotheses' after-the-fact, and to portray these 'hypotheses' falsely as having been invented beforehand. There is, of course, nothing wrong with inventing hypotheses a posteriori. There would be no point in conducting research if every scientist could formulate all possible true hypotheses a priori. What is wrong is the falsehood. For others to evaluate their work properly, scientists must speak honestly. In such a research context, the only effective way to expose inferential errors is through studies that fail to replicate prior findings and then publishing the contradictory results, but social science journals also decline to publish replications. There is also evidence that reviewers for journals support the publication of studies that are consistent with their own research and they discourage the publication of studies that contradict their own research. Since judgments about research methodology seem to play central roles in such biases, researchers are using so-called scientific methods to impede the creation of useful knowledge.

Why do people create and tolerate barriers to the creation of knowledge? Researchers very often pursue personal goals that turn knowledge creation into a symbolic facade; organizations typically place higher priority on political stability than on the validity of knowledge, and professional associations routinely endorse method rituals that foster the creation of spurious knowledge. Such behaviors suggest that people believe knowledge is not essential or unimportant. Why is there so little dissatisfaction with such behaviors? Why are such behaviors widespread and acceptable?

When a situation persists, even a situation that seems very undesirable, it is almost always the case that someone is benefiting from the situation. So who are the beneficiaries of nonprogress in the development of knowledge? It is easy to spot beneficiaries. Knowledge is power, both for the current power holders and for those who aspire to power. Students often want formulas that they can apply that will yield career success; they want proven examples and recipes to follow. Doctoral students want to believe that the research methods they are studying really do work; they want to believe that the topics discussed in journals really do matter. Dissertation committees want new theories to support their own work. Senior researchers have investments in existing methods and theories; they may even have endowed theories with their names. Senior researchers are all too aware that their high statuses depend on their mastery of the knowledge already at hand; radically new knowledge could render them obsolete and displace them from their superior positions (Starbuck 1983b).

Master Pangloss taught the metaphysico-theologico-cosmolo-nigology. He could prove to admiration that there is no effect without a cause; and, that in this best of all possible worlds, the Baron's castle was the most magnificent of all castles, and My Lady the best of all possible baronesses.

It is demonstrable, said he, that things cannot be otherwise than they are; for as all things have been created to some end, they must necessarily be created for the best end. Observe, for instance, the nose is formed for spectacles, therefore we wear spectacles. The legs are visibly designed for stockings, accordingly we wear stockings. Stones were made to be hewn, and to construct castles, therefore My Lord has a magnificent castle; for the greatest baron in the province ought to be the best lodged. Swine were intended to be eaten, therefore we eat pork all the year round; and they, who assert that everything is right, do not express themselves correctly; they should say that everything is best.

Candide listened attentively, and believed implicitly....

Voltaire (1756)

4

A Journey into Hope—Discovering Partial Solutions

This chapter resumes the report of my intellectual journey. In contrast to Chapter 2 that focused on problems, this one describes events that suggest possible solutions to these problems, or at least constructive ways to construe problems. Some events appear in both chapters because they both exposed problems and suggested solutions for problems. Again, the account is chronological.

4.1 The 1950s

As I grew increasingly fascinated with computers during my college years, my studies shifted toward electronics and applied mathematics. A topic that involves both electronics and applied mathematics is the so-called 'black-box problem'. One imagines that one is seeking to understand the behavior of an electrical circuit inside a sealed opaque box, so one can only measure electrical waves going into and out of this box. One can learn rather little about the contents of the black box by inputting a simple, steady signal, say a constant voltage at a constant frequency. However, one can learn much more by observing how the contents of the black box react to an impulse function or a step function. An impulse function is a signal that rises abruptly from nothing to something and then drops abruptly back to nothing. A step function rises abruptly from nothing to something and then remains steady. Both kinds of sudden changes induce revealing reactions. These reactions are not always sufficient to allow one to create a complete model of the circuit in the black box, but these reactions are different from and more informative than the reactions to a steady input signal.

*   *   *

Later, during my doctoral studies, a chapter by Kelley and Thibaut (1954) induced me to major in social psychology and stimulated my interest in laboratory experiments. The chapter also demonstrated that one superb article can outweigh many ordinary ones, and that a good literature review makes sense out of nonsense. Researchers had run hundreds of experiments with small groups, the results of which had been a confusing mess. Kelley and Thibaut sorted the experiments into categories, compared those in each category, and developed summary generalizations. A mess had become a configuration of answers and suggestions.

I dreamed that I might write something equally remarkable one day, and I thought I had such an opportunity when Jim March invited me to write about growth and development for his projected *Handbook of Organizations* (Starbuck 1965). I saw this invitation as the opportunity of my dreams. Not for a moment did I imagine that this book might be ignored. I worked sixteen-hour days, seven days a week, for eighteen months to write a landmark synthesis—and in fact, my chapter was very widely read and drew many citations. Thus, I always smile when I hear a researcher proclaim that success requires publishing many articles, or that empirical studies are more valuable than literature reviews. Quite the opposite is true, I believe. Nearly all empirical studies have very brief lives and insignificant influence, partly because they appear in and add to a cloud of very heterogeneous, mostly meaningless 'findings'. Readers value works that impose a degree of order on a disorderly mélange, works that seem to sift the more important from the less important.

4.2 The 1960s

Early in my years at Purdue University, I asked a senior colleague, Ed Ames, to comment on a manuscript I had drafted. After reading it, Ames gave me some writing advice. On a blackboard, he wrote what I have subsequently called Ames' law:

$$Verbs > Adverbs > Adjectives > Nouns$$

The greater-than symbols, he explained, meant 'are better than'. So, his law stated: verbs are better than adverbs, which are better than adjectives, which are better than nouns.

Ames regarded this law as a useful guide to making writing more readable and interesting, and after some experimentation, I came to agree with him. He explained that nouns make language seem lifeless, and hence boring, whereas verbs create vibrancy. If one can express an idea via a verb instead of a noun, the idea becomes a bit more interesting. As well, nouns usually foster verbosity, so if one can express an idea via a verb instead of a noun, the statement often becomes slightly more concise. Although each change has a small effect, the cumulative effect of many such changes can be rather dramatic. Here are some examples of changes that replace nouns or adjectives with verbs:

1. One focus of this research has been the identification of → This research has identified
2. Fit is the essence of design → Fit guides design (or, fit should guide design)
3. It is a system that is continuously evolving → The system evolves continuously
4. Such a classification system will be an essential building block in population-ecology models → Population ecology requires such classifications
5. The economic output of each establishment is the principal characteristic by which it is classified → Economists classify establishments principally by their economic outputs.

* * *

Around the time Ames told me how to write in a more interesting fashion, I fabricated a rule for myself that proved so valuable that I later began to call it my golden rule. A journal had sent me reviewers' comments, and as always, their comments upset me. I was complaining at least to myself and possibly to others about the reviewers' stupidity, their ignorance, their insulting language. Then I suddenly had an important insight that I phrased as follows:

No reviewer is ever wrong!

I stated the rule this extreme way mainly because the assertion appears ludicrous and bizarre. The extreme phrasing was supposed to make me stop ranting and reflect carefully. Obviously, any human being, including an editor or reviewer, may err. Sometimes, editors' or reviewers' comments seem to reveal their ignorance or stupidity, or they recommend misguided or unethical actions. Some reviewers appear to be arrogant, disrespectful, and even nasty. Therefore, asserting that reviewers are never wrong appears absurd. However, this apparent absurdity draws attention to a more fundamental truth: every editor and every reviewer is a sample from the population of potential readers. Indeed, a reviewer may have read the manuscript more carefully than most readers read published articles, and nearly every reviewer reads through an entire manuscript instead of giving up in disgust or boredom after a few pages.

My golden rule reminds me to look upon reviewers' comments not as judgments about the value of my research or the quality of my writing, but as data about how readers might react to my manuscripts. If a reviewer interprets one of my statements in a different way than I intended, other readers, possibly many other readers, are likely to interpret this statement differently than I intended; so I should revise the statement to make such misinterpretations less likely. If a reviewer thinks that I made a methodological error, other readers, possibly many of them, are likely to think that I made this error; so I should revise my manuscript to explain why my methodology is appropriate. If a reviewer recommends that I cite literature that I deem irrelevant, other readers are likely to think that this literature is relevant; so I should explain why it is irrelevant. In general, I should attend very carefully to the thoughts of anyone who may have read my words carefully. These are much more realistic data than the polite but superficial comments of close colleagues, who may have read my manuscript hastily and who do not want to hurt my feelings. Good data about readers' reactions are valuable and they can never be 'wrong'.

My golden rule does not assert that I should always follow reviewers' advice. Absolutely not! Their advice derives from their interpretations of what they thought I was trying to say, which may not be what I actually intended to say. What reviewers advise me to do often conflicts with advice I get from colleagues or from other reviewers, so I have to choose between alternative suggestions. Most of the time, reviewers' advice also conforms to widely accepted beliefs about proper methodology, and these, in my experience, are often incorrect.

* * *

Together, Ames' law and my golden rule initiated a revolution in my thinking about the publication of research. I realized that social scientists have to market their research. They need to entice people to read their articles, and they need to persuade readers that the ideas and theories in their articles are plausible and useful. Social scientists who believe that they have something valuable to contribute have to be willing to persuade others of this value; and to do that, they must adapt their manuscripts to the perceptual frameworks of potential readers. However, editors and reviewers sometimes tell authors to say some very silly things or some dishonest ones. The ultimate decisions about what is right must come from inside oneself, expressing one's own expertise, way of thinking, and ethics.

* * *

My engagement with laboratory experiments led me to a landmark article titled 'Strong Inference'. In it, Platt (1964) considered why some scientific fields, such as molecular biology and high-energy physics, make progress faster than others do, and he inferred that these fields had focused on devising crucial experiments that rule out unproductive lines of thought. That is, science has made progress in these fields mainly by showing that some hypotheses are incorrect, not by showing that 'new' hypotheses might possibly be correct (Popper 1959). Disconfirming impossible theories is much more valuable than showing support for possible theories because, 'Any conclusion that is not an exclusion is insecure and must be rechecked' (Platt 1964: 347). To qualify as a useful theory, said Platt, a proposition must exclude some possible events; if a theory predicts that anything is possible, it actually makes no meaningful predictions. Showing that a hypothesis is consistent with some observations only indicates that the hypothesis might be correct. Since many hypotheses might possibly be correct, not merely the tested hypothesis, negligible progress occurs. Indeed, research that only supports hypotheses without excluding any actually decreases knowledge by increasing ambiguity.

When I read Platt's article, I was attempting to model the processes by which people choose among probabilistic alternatives. I was considering five functional forms for the relationship between risk and return. That is, I imagined that specific mathematical functions might describe the trade-offs that people make between less risk and lower average return, or vice versa. Platt's ideas induced me to design choice alternatives that no one should choose. For example, I could design choice alternatives based on a linear relationship between risk and return. Different alternatives should look 'best' depending on a chooser's preferred trade-off between risk and return. Although each chooser would prefer one of these alternatives over the others, the three choice alternatives would span all possible preferences for the trade-offs between risk and return, so every chooser should prefer one of these three alternatives. Then I could design a fourth choice alternative that would be inferior to all three of the other alternatives. If trade-offs between risk and return were linear, no chooser would select this fourth alternative. If someone did choose this fourth alternative, it would be clear evidence that the chooser had not behaved according to a linear relationship between risk and return.

I designed around 100 choice problems such that one alternative in each problem would be inconsistent with one of the five functional forms I was considering. I presented the choice problems to three choosers. Every chooser made some choices that excluded every one of my hypothesized functional forms! If the people I had studied were making choices according to my theory, every one of them had ruled out all five of my hypotheses about the possible relationships between risk and return. Thus, I discovered that the downside of strong inference is that it may provide definitive evidence that all of your hypotheses are inadequate.

Despite my disappointment with the outcome of that experiment, I nevertheless continue to believe that Platt was right. My data excluded my hypotheses because they were inadequate hypotheses, and my empirical result convinced me that I was trying to operate within the framework of a defective theory. Specifically, I had been assuming that choices are deterministic, that people are certain to choose the alternatives that have the highest values according to their preference functions, and my five hypotheses had provided for a very wide range of possible preference functions. Subsequently, I read about and considered probabilistic theories of choice, which say that people sometimes choose alternatives that do not have the very highest values. Choice behavior acquires a probabilistic character because of the difficulties of discriminating between similar alternatives; someone who chooses between two very similar alternatives is about equally likely to choose either of them (Luce and Galanter 1963).

These issues illustrate one of the problems of applying methodological lessons from the physical sciences to the social sciences: It is extremely difficult to formulate tests that completely rule out alternative hypotheses. Because human behavior is not completely deterministic and people do make mistakes, it is possible to observe behaviors that violate valid generalizations.

* * *

My experiences with computer simulation showed the validity of Bonini's paradox—'As a model grows more realistic it also becomes just as difficult to understand as the real-world processes it represents.' Neither human brains nor the methods available to researchers can cope with serious complexity. Indeed, people (including researchers) have difficulty making sense of results when four or more variables interacted (Meehl 1954; Box and Draper 1969; Goldberg 1970; Faust 1984).

Whereas Bonini's paradox had taught me that researchers need to keep their thinking simple, I learned two additional lessons about thought from my apparent success in creating a logically satisfying theory based on data that contained large, systematic errors. Firstly, one should beware of trying to infer causal processes from the results of statistical analyses. At best, such inferences are no better than one's data and since the statistical analyses make assumptions that may be inaccurate or unjustified, such inferences may be much worse than one's data. Secondly, one should not trust one's logic. Brains exhibit great skill in making things look logical, so one needs to view logical deductions with skepticism and to develop techniques for challenging one's logical inferences (Starbuck 1983b).

* * *

My colleagues, Gerald Gordon and Sue Marquis found that medical sociologists working in properly managed, academically marginal settings—health agencies, hospitals, or medical schools—were three times as likely as their university colleagues to produce highly innovative studies. Gordon and Marquis (1966: 198–9) inferred:

Given a research environment that allows freedom of choice, many scientists choose safe rather than dangerous but original research paths. . . .

We believe that the visibility of research consequences, in addition to aiding in the location of research problems, is one of the more important factors in overcoming the resistance to innovation. For instance, in an organizational setting where the owner of an organization or his representative can accurately evaluate the findings of a project in terms of organizational goals, he can encourage the researcher who shows high probability of solving such problems. Also he can reward the researcher in relation to the extent to which the researcher aids in problem solution. As a consequence, the researcher is motivated to seek solutions to difficult but 'relevant problems' in preference to less relevant but easier problems. In seeking a solution to the difficult problems the researcher at times must abandon traditional methods and thinking. . . .

Marginal institutions, such as the medical school, hospital, and health agency, allow for more visibility of consequences than the university because they are in closer contact with the population served by the research.

4.3 The 1970s

After Howard Aldrich (1972) attempted to use path analysis to develop a causal model from data that the Aston group had gathered, Gordon Hilton (1972) responded by showing that the Aston data were consistent with three alternative theories: (a) the one advanced by the Aston group; (b) the one advanced by Aldrich; and (c) a theory that combined elements of both theories. This exchange reinforced my growing skepticism about efforts to use statistical analyses to infer relations among variables, especially causal relations, but others as well. I also saw a second, more general lesson relating to causal models: I should assume that all causal arrows have two heads.

I surmised that although there are causal relations that flow in only one direction, two-way causation is much more prevalent than one-way causation. Many phenomena that seem to involve one-way causation do so only in the short run. A influences B directly in the short run but in the long run B influences A through a feedback path. By asserting unequivocally that all causal arrows have two heads, I can force myself to search for those long-run feedbacks that I had overlooked. For example, high school grades influence colleges' admission decisions, as colleges select students with higher grades. However, colleges' admission decisions influence high school grades too. Students work to achieve higher grades in order to earn admission to their preferred colleges, and high school teachers award more high grades in order to help their students enter colleges.

* * *

My aborted attempt to simulate a division of the Koppers Company had alerted me to potential problems with spontaneous data—data that emerge from studied situations without stimulus or intervention by researchers. In Koppers, data in files at individual factories said that the factories had been less profitable than shown by the data that the factories had sent to corporate headquarters. A dozen years later, I acquired different doubts about spontaneous data after I moved to London and sat in on meetings of the Aston researchers, who saw organizations as static and generally optimal. They had gathered no data about changes, and their analytic frames assumed that they had observed effective organizational forms. I began to muse about the alternatives to spontaneous data. Where or how could researchers obtain data that would enable them to see systems as changeable or changing, as imperfect or ineffective? Should researchers be passively observing events that transpire naturally or should they be actively intervening to induce events to happen? As I saw it, trying to make events happen would be a way to test theory. I suppose this idea reflected my background in laboratory experimentation, in which researchers try to produce effects in order to test theories.

As well, experiences in which I had deceived myself by trying to make sense of data came to mind. Human minds (mine at least) seemed to be able to generate seemingly credible explanations for virtually any data. So how could people protect themselves from their agile minds? Were the risks of self-deception higher in retrospective analyses that forewarn researchers about how processes did develop? Because retrospective theories can be consistent with the prominent stylized facts, all retrospective theories appear to perform fairly well. To expose differences between theories, researchers must shift from retrospection to prediction. Of course, prediction also entails many problems including the possibility of making accurate predictions based on erroneous assumptions.

Thus, I saw two interdependent dimensions on which research methods differ. Researchers who observe phenomena retrospectively have to do so passively because one cannot intervene into the past. Researchers who attempt to intervene actively in events must formulate predictions about the outcomes of their interventions (Starbuck 1974, 1976).

Scientific fields seem consistently to begin in passive-retrospective modes. A doctor collects a patient's medical history; a geologist records earth movements and the patterns generated by past movements; an economist compiles the periodic statistics that add up to an economic history. Then they propose theories to explain what they observed—a tentative diagnosis, a conjecture about the earth's development, a macroeconomic model. Such passive-retrospective biases have advantages during a scientific field's early development. They highlight the most visible and prevalent phenomena. They lessen distortions arising from scientists' observational activities. They minimize the costs of proposing erroneous theories and thereby stimulate the invention and unbiased evaluation of alternative hypotheses. They discourage the premature rejection of partially deficient theories and promote processes of revision, modification, correction, combination, and elaboration. They weaken personal associations between specific scientists and specific observations, concepts, or philosophies. They permit standards of scientific achievement to develop in relative autonomy from extrascientific payoffs.

Nevertheless, it is important that a scientific field start to diverge from its initial passive-retrospective mode when it develops enough understanding to do so. For one thing, until the doctor acts upon one of his diagnostic conjectures and prescribes a treatment, the patient can receive no benefit. However, a field can gain several advantages that are intrinsically methodological by making predictions and intervening to influence events.

Firstly, as long as scientists perceive that the costs associated with promulgating erroneous theories are low, they have little incentive to eliminate erroneous theories and hence to discriminate carefully between better hypotheses and worse ones. Social scientists tend to hang onto defective hypotheses long after their deficiencies have become obvious; comparisons among alternative theories are rather vague and inconclusive; data measurement techniques can remain fuzzy; and social scientists generally behave as if they do not take their sciences seriously.

Secondly, autonomy from its environment sterilizes scientific development. Scientific disciplines develop social structures and codes of behavior that, for all of their fundamental virtues, can become intellectual prisons that stifle innovation, creativity, and progress. I remembered that Gordon and Marquis (1966) had found that researchers in academically marginal settings were three times as likely to produce highly innovative studies as were university researchers. This suggested that one way to prevent a progression toward sterility would be to create interactions between scientists and outsiders. Interactions with outsiders compel researchers to evaluate their methods in terms of the results they produce as judged by someone who has not been indoctrinated in the traditions of the scientific field. However, outsiders tend to want results that are useful here and now and not just retrospective interpretations of the past, and outsiders usually want useful predictions about future events.

Thirdly, an exclusive emphasis on spontaneous phenomena produces data distributions dominated by redundant, uninteresting events—nearly everyone has brown eyes, nearly all rock formations are stable, nearly all prices are the same as they were last week. To acquire data that facilitate comparisons among theories, in quantities that make these comparisons conclusive, scientists must achieve some degree of control over what they observe. At the very least, they must be able to select settings likely to yield interesting, revealing observations—meaning that they have predicted what they will observe. Moreover, to demonstrate convincingly their theories' effectiveness and completeness, they must extrapolate from past events and then intervene and engineer events that deviate from the predicted trajectories. The latter endeavors push a scientific field all the way into an active-predictive mode.

Finally, a passive-retrospective mode has limitations for analyzing people and social systems as flexible and adaptive. An adaptive system is both reactive and selectively active. It reacts to changes in and signals from its environment, and possesses a characteristic repertoire of response patterns. It also selects environmental settings to which it is capable of responding, and either learns new reaction patterns that match its environment's requirements or undertakes to modify its environment to bring its properties into line with its own capabilities (Normann 1971). To analyze such a system effectively, a researcher must strive to distinguish among and to comprehend individually a system's short-run immediately programmed reactions, its flexibilities for learning new reaction patterns or rigidities for preserving old ones, and its long-run strategies for selecting or creating appropriate environments.

Influenced by my early education in engineering, it occurred to me that researchers might be able to study adaptive systems by observing how they respond to various perturbations. Natural experiments occur when exogenous events displace social systems from their normal equilibria. In these situations, one can see some of systems' adaptive and reactive capabilities, which opens the possibility of discovering why equilibria exist. If they could control the situations that social systems confront, researchers might observe reactions to regular oscillatory inputs of different frequencies, to sudden steplike shocks, to informational noise, or to disruptions of internal and external information channels. Such perturbations would reveal properties that are not evident when the system is in equilibrium. However, such perturbations do not often occur spontaneously, so researchers must either have good luck or they must intervene and exert a degree of control over what happens. Interventions force researchers to make predictions and to reflect about their values because people demand plausible forecasts of the consequences of proposed interventions and they place evaluations on alternative interventions.

* * *

During my time in Berlin in the early 1970s, I read an article, or possibly a book review, that criticized use of the verb 'to be'. The article argued that writers not only overuse 'to be' but that use of this verb renders language static and less interesting. 'To be' eliminates change and implies equilibrium. 'The company is profitable' seems to describe a stable property of the company, not the outcome of a developmental process or an attribute that might disappear. Obviously, each such phrase is innocuous, but when authors create sentence after sentence with 'to be' verbs, the effect accumulates. Language becomes more lively and appealing when authors use active verbs instead of 'to be'. 'The company is making profits' would be somewhat more lively than 'The company is profitable' but neither does it describe a developmental path, as would 'The company has learned how to make a profit', nor does it suggest uncertainty, as would 'The company made a profit this year'.

This focus on a commonplace element in everyday language intrigued me. For one thing, use of 'to be' as an auxiliary verb generally indicates lively language: 'The company is profiting from its new products'. For another thing, passive verbs, which resemble 'to be' followed by an adjective, generally deaden language, whereas active verbs generally enliven language. 'The company is made profitable by its new products' is both more verbose and less involving than 'New products made the company profitable'. Thus, I revised Ames' law by adding a distinction between active and passive verbs:

Active verbs > Adverbs > Adjectives > Nouns > Passive verbs

Active verbs are better than adverbs, which are better than adjectives, which are better than nouns, which are better than passive verbs.

I adopted this modified rule with the intention of making my writing more interesting and readable. Therefore, I was surprised to discover that it was altering the way I thought. I was no longer satisfied with the same kinds of theoretical propositions, and some statements I had written earlier made me cringe. The obvious way to use active verbs is to identify sources of action and to make these actors the subjects of sentences. As a result, I had to attend constantly to causality and to explicate causal processes that I had previously left implicit. My theories grew clearer, and they also grew more dynamic.

There is, however, an obvious parallel between the need to explicate causal processes in order to use active verbs and the need to explicate causal processes in order to create simulation models. I knew that this pressure had induced some simulators to invent the details that they did not have, so I tried to avoid making a similar mistake.

My newfound consciousness of active and passive verbs stimulated me to watch the ways other people were using verbs. I surmised that passive verbs and nouns encourage social scientists to view themselves as passive observers, to see other people as puppets of impersonal forces, and to build static theories. Using static words to describe reality leads scientists to create static frames of reference, to view social worlds as stable, and thus to overlook dynamic events. Using active verbs and adverbs, on the other hand, subtly encourages scientists to notice changes, reactions, developmental processes, and histories, and to see themselves as actual and potential actors.

*　*　*

Wolfgang Müller and I tried to help the German Health Administration to design an information system that would help them assess the effectiveness of new medications. These contacts led to an invitation to give statistical advice to doctors in Ulm who were hunting for side effects of contraceptive pills. One result was our finding out that doctors are the most important 'predictors' of ailments: according to the data from this study, the strongest correlates of side effects were the identities of the women's doctors. Some doctors reported coronary problems, some reported respiratory problems, some reported gastrointestinal problems, and so on. Again, spontaneous data had deceptive properties.

A more profound result of this activity was a conversation that eventually became one of the most important of my life. The conversation reinforced my conviction that efforts to intervene into events would strengthen the social sciences generally, and management and organization theory more specifically (Starbuck 1993a). The doctor with whom I spoke challenged the conventional idea that one needs to understand a system before one dares to try to change it. Indeed, the doctor's views, which I later adopted as my own, suggest that to understand a complex, dynamic system, one must try to change it and observe how it reacts.

After we had spent several hours discussing statistical issues of their contraception project, the doctor who headed the project asked what research we ourselves were doing. I told him I was trying to write a computer program to help doctors make medical diagnoses.

He probed, 'Why do you want to do that?'

Surprised to hear this question from a doctor, I explained, 'I want to improve medical care.'

'But, better diagnosis would not improve medical care', he countered, 'because diagnosis is not important to *good* medical care.' He put a lot of stress on that adjective 'good'.

I could not believe what I was hearing. 'Wait a minute', I protested. 'Doctors base treatments on diagnoses, so more accurate diagnoses should produce better treatments. Computers can take more factors into account than doctors can, and computers overlook nothing.'

'You're wrong in assuming that diagnoses determine treatments' effectiveness', he replied. '*Good* doctors do not rely on diagnoses.'

'Yet, medical schools teach doctors to make diagnoses', I protested. 'Doctors are taught to translate symptoms into diagnoses and then to base treatments on diagnoses.'

'That's right. Medical schools do teach that', the doctor admitted, 'but the doctors who do what they were taught in medical school never become *good* doctors.

'There are many more combinations of symptoms than there are diagnoses, so translating symptoms into diagnoses discards information. Moreover, there are many more treatments than diagnoses, so basing treatments on diagnoses injects random errors. Doctors can

Symptoms   Diagnoses   Treatments

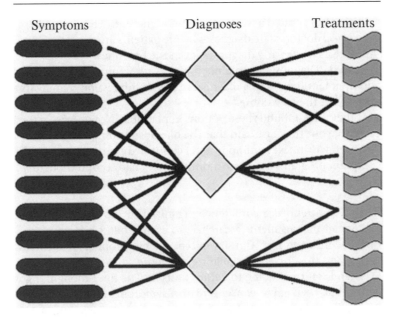

Figure 4.1 Why diagnosis impedes treatment

make more dependable links between symptoms and treatments if they leave diagnoses out of the chain.'

Figure 4.1 illustrates how this doctor perceived relations among symptoms, diagnoses, and treatments.

'However', the doctor continued, 'the links between symptoms and treatments are not the most important keys to finding effective treatments. *Good* doctors pay careful attention to how patients respond to treatments. If a patient gets better, current treatments are heading in the right direction. However, current treatments often do not work or they produce side effects that require correction. The model of symptoms–diagnoses–treatments ignores the feedback loop from treatments to symptoms, but this feedback loop is the most important factor in successful treatment.

'Doctors should not take diagnoses seriously because strong expectations can keep them from noticing important reactions. Of course, over time, sequences of treatments and their effects produce evidence about the causes of symptoms. This evidence may lead to valid diagnoses by the time treatment ends.'

I thought I spotted a weak spot in his argument. 'Then, why do so-called *good* doctors state diagnoses before patients are cured?', I asked. 'All doctors make early diagnoses, even the best ones.'

He said, 'Diagnoses are mainly useful as something to tell patients and their families. Stating diagnoses gives an impression that doctors know what they are doing.'

At that time, I found these notions implausible. Not only were they eccentric, but they also said that the diagnostic computer program I had been writing was unimportant. I continued trying to develop the computer program, but some months later, I had second thoughts.

* * *

In 1972, I attended a conference organized to introduce American and Soviet management researchers to each other. I had never ventured behind the Iron Curtain except for brief tourist trips to East Berlin, and this trip was fascinating and tense.

When I returned home to Berlin, I was ill. The flu, I thought. I got better, but then grew worse, and the symptoms seemed stronger. Again, I got better and then the symptoms returned. And again. And again. Each cycle produced stronger symptoms. One day two months later, I realized that I was crawling on my hands and knees up the stairs to my office because I could barely breathe.

I asked an ENT doctor if I had hay fever. The symptoms seemed stronger when I read my son bedtime stories. One of my grandfathers had had asthma, the other severe hay fever, and my father hay fever. Might I be reacting to the straw in my son's guinea pig cage?

The doctor said I needed sinus surgery and sent me to a surgeon. A few days after the operation, I went home feeling good for the first time in two months.

However, after a week, my breathing problems resumed. The surgeon sent me back to the hospital. The resident doctors sent samples to a lab, which identified a bacterial infection that penicillin could cure. Massive doses of penicillin made digestion impossible, and I lost thirty pounds in two weeks. For the first time in years, I weighed what the charts recommended. The penicillin also seemed to cure my infection. I felt fine, and the doctors sent me home.

Again, after a week, my breathing problems resumed. After two weeks, I stopped breathing almost entirely. The crisis came on abruptly one evening. With help from a university student who lived in our basement, my wife bundled me into the auto and drove pell-mell with the horn blowing to the nearest hospital. I was nearly unconscious, but I think I remember white-coated people clamping a mask on my face and injecting my arms.

This time the doctors tried treating me with tetracycline because it killed bacteria that penicillin missed, and some viruses. After another two weeks, I went home again feeling fine.

Then, after a few days, I stopped breathing almost entirely. Again, we made a high-speed trip to the emergency room and I had vague images of white coats working over me.

When I awoke the next day, I lit a cigarette as usual. For twenty years, I had smoked two to three packs a day. That morning, one of my doctors walked into the hospital room, pointed at my cigarette and declared sternly, '*That* is what is killing you!'

I believed him. I put out the cigarette and have not smoked since. Unfortunately, smoking was not really what was killing me. I suffered more breathing crises. We repeated the emergency trips for four months.

I did not find the repetition boring, however. My doctors were running out of hypotheses and treatments. The cycles were growing shorter, the trips to the hospital more frequent.

My doctors sent me to Germany's most famous allergist, whom I cherish as a prototype of ascribed expertise. I told him my hypothesis about the straw in my son's guinea pig cage. He injected several different kinds of sera in each of my arms, looked at the reactions and announced that I had no important allergies. None at all. I pointed out that my right arm had swelled up to twice its normal diameter. The allergist explained, 'It is nothing significant! What do you expect after all the things I injected?'

Thereafter, I had no allergies in Germany. The ultimate authority had so stated. Other doctors refused to entertain the possibility.

One day, two of my doctors came together to my bedside and advised me that I should anticipate dying. They explained they did not know why I had asthma or how to prevent it. They had run out of ideas. The crises would certainly recur. Experience indicated that a hospital could probably revive me; but one day, I would not reach a hospital in time. Therefore, I should try to enjoy what remained of my life, which might be only a few weeks.

Having gone through eight months of escalating evidence that something was seriously wrong, I believed them and went home to die. I was 38.

I tried to figure out what to do with my remaining days, but I felt too sick to do anything useful. I did not even compose a will. I mostly stayed in bed because I had so much trouble breathing. I also noticed that I was paying more attention to my impending death than anyone else was.

My wife watched me for a few days. Then she declared, 'If you're going to die, it is not going to be at home in bed! You had better die in a doctor's office, trying to find out what is wrong with you.'

I thought she was heartless and unsympathetic, but I also thought she was speaking sense.

I telephoned John Dutton, whose sister worked for a famous doctor in Boston. After making inquiries, he told me to go to Mayo Clinic in Minnesota.

When I got to Mayo, I no longer had symptoms. None whatever! I was quite embarrassed and afraid the doctors would neither believe how ill I had been nor be able to discover why I had been ill.

However, their tests disclosed allergies. Technicians carefully measured the amount of each substance injected, monitored the time for a reaction to develop with a stopwatch, and measured the amount of reaction with a micrometer. Then they consulted statistical tables and translated my reactions into standard deviations. My reactions to most furs and feathers were two standard deviations above normal. My reactions to guinea pig fur were off the chart, which stopped at five standard deviations.

I believe that I have proven beyond all doubt that surgery, penicillin, and tetracycline are ineffective treatments for an allergy to guinea pigs. These treatments and others had appeared to work solely because I was not at home, where my son had a guinea pig and I had a cage of finches. Staying in a hotel would have been an effective treatment for my allergies as long as the hotel did not have feather pillows or fur rugs.

* * *

While I was lying in a hospital bed believing I was going to die, an editor had come to visit me. He asked if I was writing a book that his company might publish. I was impressed by the effort he had taken to search me out in a hospital, but I was busy being quite ill. I thanked him for his interest and promised to contact him if I did write a book...which seemed very unlikely.

Months in bed believing I was going to die had induced serious stocktaking. I had experienced at firsthand the deficiencies of post hoc analyses and theorizing, I had been mulling over my conversation with the doctor in Ulm and I had seen diverse versions of medical diagnosis in practice. The views of the doctor in Ulm made more and more sense to me.

Academic research is trying to follow a model like that taught in medical schools. Scientists are translating data into theories, and promising to develop prescriptions from the theories. Data are like symptoms, theories like diagnoses, and prescriptions like treatments. Are not social systems as dynamic as human bodies and similarly complex? Theories do not capture all the information in data, and they do not determine prescriptions uniquely. Perhaps scientists could establish stronger links between data and prescriptions if they did not insert theories between them. Indeed, should not data be the results of prescriptions? Should not theories derive from observing relations between prescriptions and subsequent data?

I conjectured that active interventions both might help researchers to achieve more complete, dynamic understanding of people and social systems. The systems social scientists are trying to understand are very complex and flexible, perhaps too complex and flexible for traditional research methods that rely on spontaneous data and static analyses. But if we have to change people and social systems in order to understand them, the phenomena I had once thought of as objective 'realities' ought to be partly products of our research. This raises issues about what it might mean to 'improve' the objects of study, to prescribe.

Remembering the editor who had come to visit me in the hospital, I began to think about writing a book that would advance the idea of using prescriptions for studies of organizations. I imagined a book that would persuade organization theorists to practice prescriptive science instead of descriptive. I was not convinced that organization theorists should actually make interventions because researchers lack training in prescription and experience with doing it (Czarniawska 2001). However, researchers could offer suggestions about how to make organizations 'better'.

I wrote to the editor who had visited me in the hospital. He replied that they were very interested; could I submit an outline? The outline had eighty chapters and implied a book with more words than the Bible. It would take me years to write, and I obviously could not count on living for years. Moreover, I wanted to change research practices, not publish a manifesto. I could better foster change by enlisting coauthors—many of them and strategically chosen. Therefore, I proposed a book with eighty authors, a *Handbook of Organizational Design* (Nystrom and Starbuck 1981). As the editors of this handbook, Nystrom and I discovered that many academic authors find it very difficult to think about what might be 'better'.

* * *

Just before I moved back to the USA in 1974, I attended a conference in Mexico and took advantage of a tour package offered in connection with the conference. Before departing for Mexico, I read a travel guide that warned tourists not to drink water from faucets. Therefore, for two weeks, I carefully restricted myself to the bottled water that every hotel room provided.

Near midnight on a very hot night in Merida, Yucatan, I drank the last of my bottled water. I took my bottle down to the desk clerk and asked if he could get me more.

He said, 'I will be happy to help you as soon as I am finished, but you are welcome to get the water yourself.'

'I don't mind getting the water myself', I answered. 'Where is it?'

'Just fill the bottle at that faucet over there', he instructed.

'You mean this is just ordinary water from the faucet! Why do you put it in bottles?'

'Tourists refuse to drink it unless it is in bottles', he explained.

The acceptance of ideas depends on how one frames them.

* * *

My studies with Bo Hedberg and Paul Nystrom demonstrated how teamwork can alter one's thinking. Our collaboration sprang initially from an argument. Whereas Hedberg wanted to find out why some industries stagnate and drive companies out of business, I wondered why smart managers keep their companies in stagnating industries. I perceived industrial stagnation as posing problems for the managers of individual companies, whereas Hedberg perceived industrial stagnation as posing problems for government policies.

We eventually resolved our disagreement by concluding that both of us had been partly right. We gradually stopped talking about stagnating environments and spoke increasingly of organizations facing crises. Crises result partly from organization's environments, although not quite as Hedberg had initially conceived. Environments do change so as to make markets, products, and technologies obsolete, but environments also endorse prescriptions about how to organize that make it hard for organizations to adapt to environmental changes. Crises also result partly from properties of organizations, but somewhat differently than I had conceived at first. Organizations do make mistakes, but they also strive to stabilize their environments and they blind themselves to environmental events that deviate from their expectations. Our most important finding was an idea that neither of us had imagined initially: Serious crises result from exactly the same causal processes that produce great successes (Starbuck, Greve, and Hedberg 1978; Starbuck 1989).

Hegel would have been proud of us. Our joint research showed how two viewpoints that appeared at first to be completely antithetical could synthesize into a broader integrated understanding. Our minds are entirely too quick to see only a portion of a situation and to lock in on incomplete interpretations. We need to tear ourselves free from narrow thinking and to consider alternatives. Debates between collaborators can help researchers to clarify concepts, and dialectical reasoning can help researchers to break out of the mental prisons they build with rationality. Collaborative research can foster dialectical reasoning by framing issues as conflicts and then encouraging the collaborators to discover gradually that the conflicts can be resolved by framing situations more generally.

* * *

Researchers sometimes portray as significant insights the differences between correlations computed over different units of analysis. Studies by Hatten and Schendel (1977) and by Schendel and Patton (1978) brought this issue to my attention. Hatten and Schendel (1977) analyzed statistical data about American brewing companies and concluded that these differ from one another. They proposed that these companies form 'strategic groups'. Then, Schendel and Patton (1978) divided brewing companies into three categories—small regional, large regional, and national—and computed separate regression coefficients for each category. Figure 4.2 graphs their basic finding. As they (1978: 1616) put it, 'at the industry level, increasing market share was found to have a significant positive effect on profitability. . . . For each subgroup the relationship was found to be negative'. A decade later, Cool and Schendel (1988) observed that individual

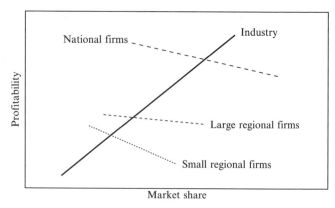

Figure 4.2 Profitability versus market share of US brewers
(Source: Schendel and Patton 1978)

companies may differ from the other members of their strategic groups, and indeed, that these relationships may change over time, so neither the industry-level graph nor the group-level graphs made statements relevant for individual companies.

*   *   *

Sometime during the late 1970s or early 1980s, I became aware of Pygmalion effects, in which predictions affect outcomes. Predictions may become either self-fulfilling or self-denying. These effects weaken even further the usefulness of retrospective research. Although explaining the past may reassure us and comfort us, it may also do little to help us influence our futures. Pygmalion effects also confront us with the issue of what realities we wish to understand—the ones that did exist when we gathered data or the ones that might exist after we attempt to exert influence.

4.4 The 1980s

Around 1980, Alan Meyer introduced me to triangulation, which means using more than one type of methodology to investigate a situation (Denzin 1978; Jick 1979). Meyer had just completed a study of some hospitals and was writing his analysis when doctors in that area went on strike to protest a dramatic increase in their insurance premiums (Meyer 1982*a*, 1982*b*). He decided to go back to the hospitals and observe how they reacted to the strike. Since he had been studying them, he thought that he could predict their reactions, so he was very surprised that they were not behaving as he had expected. A professor advised Meyer not to rely on questionnaires because that would be asking people to describe their efforts to react even as they were trying to puzzle out what to do; he should go into the hospitals and observe behaviors himself. Thus, Meyer ended up with several kinds of data—accounting data, questionnaires, interviews, and personal observations—and he had to integrate these diverse perspectives. His analysis was widely cited and admired in part because he had integrated diverse data and he had shown how quantitative and qualitative data could complement each other. In particular, he demonstrated that correlations calculated across 19 hospitals were consistent with his observations in case studies.

* * *

Karl Weick entered my life again to tell me to read an article by Murray Davis titled 'That's interesting!' Davis (1971: 309) asserted,

It has long been thought that a theorist is considered great because his theories are true, but this is false. A theorist is considered great, not because his theories are true, but because they are interesting. Those who carefully and exhaustively verify trivial theories are soon forgotten, whereas those who cursorily and expediently verify interesting theories are long remembered. In fact, the truth of a theory has very little to do with its impact, for a theory can continue to be found interesting even though its truth is disputed—even refuted!

He then proceeded to propose twelve patterns that typify interesting theories. All of these patterns have the property that they first advance a proposition and then contradict it. For example, 'what seems to be an independent variable is in reality a dependent variable', or 'what seem to be opposite phenomena are in reality nearly identical phenomena', or 'what seem to be unrelated phenomena are in reality interdependent phenomena'.

Davis' article drove home to me the importance of selling one's ideas to readers. I realized that successful writing is not only a matter of clear explanation but also involves presenting ideas in ways that readers find intriguing or attractive. The article also made me aware that authors who want their ideas to have wide influence have to give their ideas away by denying personal ownership of them and allowing readers to own them. An author who speaks of 'my theory' or 'my hypothesis' makes it a bit more difficult for readers to adopt that theory or hypothesis because the author owns these.

* * *

From the mid-1970s to the mid-1980s, Nystrom and I cotaught a course titled 'Advanced Organization Design' for executive MBA students. The title was somewhat misleading in that the course really focused on solving real-life organizational problems. Alone or in small groups, the executive MBA students identified problems, designed change efforts, attempted the change efforts, monitored the results, analyzed what had happened, and then designed new change efforts. The problems ranged from coping with a difficult subordinate to reorienting a division. I learned more than any of the students because I watched 150 such efforts over ten years, and I found the experience quite interesting.

The structure of 'Advanced Organization Design' reflected the ideas of the doctor from Ulm. Although the students needed to analyze the problematic situations before taking actions, I urged them to formulate and initiate their action plans quickly so that they would have time to monitor the reactions to their actions during the period of the course. My premise was that the reactions to their actions might reveal more about why the problems existed. Although they often did not actually solve the problems within the course's three-month span, they generally developed much better understanding of the problems by the time the course ended.

'Advanced Organization Design' relied heavily on a fascinating book by Watzlawick, Weakland, and Fisch (1974). They had set up a center for treating psychiatric problems with 'brief therapy', and they had had remarkable success in solving problems after only a few hours of therapy. Their basic premise was that problems take root in perceptions. Problems exist because people perceive situations to be problematic, and problems are unsolvable because perceptions make them so. All perceptual frameworks have blind spots that prevent people from solving certain kinds of problems and that link behaviors into self-reinforcing cycles. In many cases, these cycles occur because someone is benefiting from the existence of the problems. In other cases, problems persist because blind spots make the problems unsolvable. Thus, Watzlawick, Weakland, and Fisch proposed various strategies for reframing situations so that people would see them differently. The reframing may enable people to see situations that they previously deemed problematic as having unrecognized benefits that render them unproblematic, or it may enable people to see insurmountable obstacles as surmountable. Since the problems persist in the first place because logical problem solving is inadequate to solve them, effective solutions often involve taking actions that appear illogical within the conceptual frameworks that made the problems unsolvable. In other words, the fact that a problem appears to be unsolvable can provide useful clues about how to solve it.

* * *

I also learned a lot from teaching forecasting. Forecasting studies have repeatedly produced findings that surprised researchers, as what has worked in practice has often been quite different from what theory asserted ought to work well. I draw two important general inferences from studies of forecasting techniques. Firstly, researchers who want to make useful statements about the present and immediate future should pay much less attention to explaining what did happen in the past. Secondly, simpler theories are more robust than more complex theories, and simpler methodologies produce more robust findings than more complex methodologies do.

The vast majority of social science research can be classified as the study of history: All empirical data describe past events, and analyses of data discuss only these past events. Researchers almost never attempt to extrapolate their analyses into the future or even into the present. Indeed, researchers often make no effort to assess what changes were occurring during the recent past. Because tests of theories' adequacy rely solely on data from the past, the theories tend to have serious defects as descriptions of the future and possibly the present.

Even cross-section studies are snapshots from changing time series, so relating data about the past to current or future events is implicitly a form of time series analysis. The great majority of social and economic time series have high autocorrelations, and these autocorrelations constrain what one can usefully say about the series. Indeed, the great majority of social and economic time series are consistent with a model that says

$$S(t) = \text{Constant}^*S(t-1) + \text{Constant} + \text{Random change}$$

That is, each new value of a series has three components: (*a*) a fraction of the immediately preceding value that makes the series depend inertially on itself; (b) a change that is the same in each period and that produces a long-term linear trend; and (c) a change that is entirely random. Inertial carryover from previous periods causes random changes in prior periods to have persistent repercussions in later periods. As a result, random perturbations do not have only immediate effects; random perturbations change the bases for future events. For example, an earthquake does not merely affect earnings and capital expenditures during the period when it occurs. An earthquake has effects for several periods because economic activities in one period influence those in ensuing periods.

Pervasive high autocorrelations make it possible for forecasters to generate accurate short-range predictions with linear functions that take account only of past values of a single series and that ignore interactions among series. A forecast that assumes a long-term linear trend is likely to be quite accurate if it also takes account of the one or two most recent observations, and a forecast that ignores a long-term trend is likely to be quite accurate if it takes account of several recent observations. Dawes and Corrigan (1974) explained that it is normally useful to assume linear relations among variables because linear functions can approximate all of the functions that vary monotonically with each independent variable. Monotonic functions tend to look more linear when variables contain larger measurement errors because the errors create scatter that obscures curvature and makes all variables look more similar. As a result, a complex forecasting method has to be quite effective in order to produce more accurate forecasts than a simple linear function does.

To me, the foregoing observations have two implications. Firstly, researchers should be correcting their data to allow for linear trends. Figure 4.3 illustrates my point in a highly stylized fashion. Researchers often ignore trends and make observations at only one time. As a result, research studies are out-of-date by the time analyses are complete, and studies' findings may seriously misrepresent future situations. Since many time series change linearly in the short run, researchers could easily extrapolate their analyses to the present or immediate future.

Secondly, researchers should be testing theories by comparing them with simple alternatives. Because comparisons with null hypotheses do not test forecasting methods to any meaningful degree, forecasting researchers typically compare forecasting methods with 'naive forecasts'. For example, a naive person might advance either of two

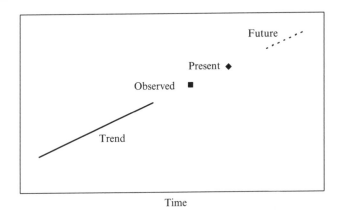

Figure 4.3 How observed data misrepresent the present and future

hypotheses about a time series. One naive hypothesis—the no-change hypothesis—says that the next value will be the same as the current value. This hypothesis makes no specific assertions about the causal processes that generate the series. It merely expresses the idea that most causal processes are inertial: What happens tomorrow will resemble what is happening today. The second naive hypothesis—the linear-trend hypothesis—says that the trend observed since yesterday will continue until tomorrow: The next value will differ from the current value by the same amount that the current value differs from the previous value. This hypothesis expresses the idea that most causal processes are inertial in trend as well as in state. Neither of these naive hypotheses says anything profound. Either could come from a young child who has no understanding of the causal processes that generate a series. Therefore, one should demand more accurate predictions from a complicated forecasting technique—or from a supposedly profound theory.

Elliott (1973) and Brodie and de Kluyver (1987) found complex forecasting models to be about as accurate as simple, naive models. However, these researchers examined only very short-range forecasts. In theory, longer-range forecasts might produce larger differences in accuracy and show larger advantages for complex methods. Makridakis and colleagues compared twenty-one to twenty-four methods while forecasting 1,001 time series relating to business (Makridakis and Hibon 1979; Makridakis et al. 1982). Although they generated forecasts for as many as eighteen periods, these researchers too found very small accuracy differences between simple methods and complex ones. In contradiction to conventional wisdom, they also found that simple, naive forecasts became a bit more likely to beat the other methods as the forecast horizons grew longer (Makridakis et al. 1982: Tables 6 and 7).

Complex forecasting methods try to extract too much information from data. The least accurate methods are generally ones that attempt to spot abrupt changes in long-term trends—turning points or re-orientations. Any method that responds promptly to sudden changes in trends also responds strongly to random events. Makridakis and Hibon (1979) noted that the methods that spot turning points more often also make large errors more often.

When one starts to ask that theories have relevance for the present and immediate future, one begins to see why complex theories and elegant analytic methods are actually misleading. Makridakis and Winkler (1983) found that an average of forecasts made by five or six methods frequently proves more accurate than *any* of its component forecasts (Winkler and Makridakis 1983; Winkler 1984). Averaging forecasts also reduces the variance of forecast errors and so makes large errors less likely. Many other studies have shown gains from averaging diverse forecasts (Armstrong 1985: 183–5; Clemen 1989). However, Makridakis reported that some professional forecasters have had trouble accepting these findings because they imply 'that there is no such thing as a best model'. Suppose that one can always improve the forecasts from a 'best' model by averaging them with the forecasts from what seems to be an inferior model. Then it must be that the 'best' model is not better than the inferior one. The apparent differences in models' accuracies must represent random errors, and valid information must be limited to elements that are shared by both models. Evidently, forecasting methods tend to mistake noise for information, and averaging several forecasts mitigates this propensity. Methods that treat random noise differently make errors that differ randomly, and averaging such forecasts pits the differing errors against each other.

A general law seems to be at work: For making statements about the present and future, more complex, subtle, or elegant techniques give no greater accuracy than simple, crude, or naive ones. Complex causal analyses rarely prove to be more accurate than simple extrapolations. Evidently, complex analytic models and complex forecasting techniques try to extract too much information from data. Although methodological theories may say that more complex methods can exploit data more fully, complex methods tend to mistake noise for information. Whether with simple or complex methods, it is normally useful to apply several methods and to average their results.

* * *

Having discovered the lessons of forecasting, I could see many reasons why very simple, naive hypotheses should be more realistic than complicated hypotheses about human reasoning or causal processes. Although people devote time and effort to developing intelligent actions, their actions very often do not yield the benefits they anticipated. In particular, humans often pursue illusory opportunities (Starbuck 1994). Consider an organization that is competing against others. The organization perceives an opportunity and moves to exploit it. If only one organization were to act alone, this opportunity might yield benefits. However, communication and imitation convert the opportunity into an illusion, and organizations that try to exploit the opportunity end up no better off—perhaps worse off—because their competitors also pursued the same opportunity (Van Valen 1973; Campbell 1985; Barnett and Hansen 1996).

Two theories of organizational growth have emphasized illusory opportunities. Andrews (1949) pointed out that business firms might expand to obtain short-run cost savings that never become real. From a short-run perspective, managers perceive some costs as 'fixed', meaning that they will not change if the amount of output goes up or down incrementally. Because these fixed costs appear to create opportunities to produce somewhat more output without incurring proportional costs, managers expect average cost per unit to decrease as output rises. Yet over the long run, all costs do vary with output, so the long-run cost per unit might stay constant or even increase as output goes up. Thus, managers might endlessly and erroneously expand output because they expect growth to decrease average cost whereas growth is actually increasing the average cost.

Similarly, Penrose (1959: 2) contrasted short-run and long-run perspectives, but she argued, 'There may be advantages in moving from one position to another quite apart from the advantages of being in a different position.' She (1959: 103) wrote, 'The growth of firms may be consistent with the most efficient use of society's resources; the result of past growth—the size attained at any time—may have no corresponding advantages. Each successive step in its growth may be profitable to the firm and, if otherwise underutilized resources are used, advantageous to society. But once any expansion is completed, the original justification for the expansion may fade into insignificance as new opportunities for growth develop and are acted upon'. This argument resembles Andrews' but Penrose also points out that the environmental situation that existed when a firm decided to expand may no longer exist by the time an expansion has been completed. The decision makers who guide firms may persistently lag behind the environments they are trying to exploit.

Fruitless behavior also occurs when people and organizations try to solve unsolvable problems. Unsolvable problems exist because people have incompatible desires or because societies espouse values that are mutually inconsistent. Since organizations embody societal values, they are trying perpetually to satisfy inconsistent demands, and organizational properties that uphold some values conflict with properties that uphold contrary values.

Hierarchical dominance affords an example. Western societies advocate democracy and equality among people, but they also advocate hierarchical control, unity of action, and efficiency. People in Western societies generally expect organizations to adopt hierarchical structures and to use these structures to coordinate actions and to eliminate waste. However, hierarchical control is undemocratic and unequal. Everyone understands why subordinates do not do as their superiors dictate, and everyone also understands why organizations have to eliminate this inefficient disunity. Therefore, organizations try to solve the 'problem' of resistance to hierarchical control—by making hierarchical control less visible or by aligning subordinates' goals with superiors' goals. In the late 1940s, the solution was for managers to manage 'democratically'. However, after a while, most subordinates inferred that their superiors' democracy was insincere, and this solution failed. In the early 1950s, the solution was for managers to exhibit 'consideration' while nevertheless controlling task activities. However, after a while, most subordinates inferred that their superiors' consideration was insincere, and this solution failed. In the late 1950s, the solution was Management-By-Objectives, in which superiors and subordinates were to meet periodically and to formulate mutually agreed goals for the subordinates. However, after a while, most subordinates inferred that their superiors were using these meetings to dictate goals, and this solution failed. In the 1960s, the solution was 'participative management', in which workers' representatives were to participate in managerial boards that made diverse decisions about methods, investments, staffing, strategies, and so on. But after a while, most workers inferred: (*a*) that managers were exerting great influence upon these boards' decisions; and (*b*) that the workers' representatives were benefiting personally from their memberships in these boards, and this solution failed. In the early 1980s, the solution was 'organizational culture', by which organizations were to produce unity of goals and methods. However, after a while, most managers learned that general solidarity did not translate into operational goals and methods, and employees resisted homogenization, and this solution failed. In the late 1980s, the solution became 'quality circles', which broadened into 'total quality management'. However, after a while, . . .

Thus, one fad has followed another. From a short-run perspective, many organizations have adopted very similar 'solutions'; and from a long-run perspective, many organizations have adopted loosely similar 'solutions'. Although the various solutions have affected superior–subordinate relations, these effects have been negative as often as positive, and the fundamental 'problem' persists. Long-run changes in the fundamental problem and in the various solutions seem to have arisen from economics, education, social structure, and technologies rather than from intraorganizational practices. From a very long-run perspective, organizations seem to have tried a series of unsuccessful practices.

* * *

Both my effort to assess progress in industrial–organizational psychology and my experience with forecasting made me an attentive audience for the debates among bioecologists about alternatives to null hypotheses. If some bioecologists could see the value of an alternative to null hypotheses, perhaps some social scientists could too. However, I think that the terminology of forecasting researchers—'naive models'—may be better than bioecologists' term 'null models' because these alternative hypotheses do incorporate some elementary assumptions.

* * *

125

Jane Webster and I (1988) brooded over the lack of progress in industrial–organizational psychology. Why is there so little agreement among psychologists about what they know? We found that studies of progress in the physical sciences emphasize the strong effects of social construction (Sullivan 1928; Latour and Woolgar 1979; Knorr-Cetina 1981; Latour 1987). Although physical scientists do discard theories that do not work, the scientists themselves exercise a good deal of choice when they decide whether theories work. Their social interactions affect the aspects of phenomena that the theories are supposed to explain and the criteria researchers use to gauge theories' efficacies.

Newton's laws are one of the best-known substantive paradigms. Physicists came to accept these laws because they enabled better predictions concerning certain phenomena, but the laws say nothing whatever about some properties of physical systems, and the laws fail to explain some phenomena that physicists have expected them to explain, such as light or subatomic interactions. In no sense are Newton's laws absolute truths. Rather they are statements that physicists use as baselines for explanation: Physicists attempt to build explanations upon Newton's laws first. If these explanations work, the physicists are satisfied, and they have renewed confidence in Newton's laws. If these baseline explanations do not work, physicists try to explain the deviations from Newton's laws. Are there, for instance, previously unnoticed exogenous influences? Finally, if some inexplicable deviations from Newton's laws recur systematically, but only in this extreme circumstance, physicists contemplate alternative theories, e.g. Einstein's theory of relativity.

The contrast to social science is striking... and suggestive. The difference between physics and social science may be more in the minds of physicists and social scientists than in the phenomena they study (Landy and Vasey 1984). After arguing that social science facts are approximately as stable over time as physical ones, Hedges (1987: 453–4) contrasted physical and social science theories as follows:

New physical theories are not sought on every occasion in which there is a modest failure of experimental consistency. Instead, reasons for the inconsistency are likely to be sought in the methodology of the research studies. At least tentative confidence in theory stabilizes the situation so that a rather extended series of inconsistent results would be required to force a major reconceptualization. In social sciences, theory does not often play this stabilizing role.

Campbell (1982: 697) characterized the theories of psychology as 'collections of statements that are so general that asserting them to be true conveys very little information'. However, of course, the same observation applies to the major propositions of the physical sciences such as Newton's laws: Any truly general proposition can convey no information about where it applies because it applies everywhere, and of course, any proposition that is always true must be tautological (Smedslund, 1984). General theoretical propositions are heuristic guidelines rather than formulae with obvious applications in specific instances, and it is up to scientists to apply these heuristics in specific instances.

However, general theoretical propositions are more than just heuristics because they serve social functions as well. Scientific progress is a perception by scientists, and theories need not be completely correct in order to aid scientific progress. As much as correctness, theories need the backing of consensus and consistency. When scientists agree among themselves to explain phenomena in terms of baseline theories, they project their findings into shared perceptual frameworks that reinforce the collective nature of research by facilitating communication and comparison and by defining what is important or irrelevant. Indeed, insofar as science is a collective enterprise, abstractions do not become theoretical propositions until they win widespread social support. A lack of substantive consensus is equivalent to a lack of theory, and scientists must agree to share a theory in order to build on each other's work. Making progress depends upon scientists' agreeing to make progress.

Webster and I (1988) proposed some propositions about industrial–organizational psychology that illustrate the kinds of baseline theoretical propositions that would help social scientists to move forward. These propositions describe various phenomena and deviations from them point to contingencies. For example, we proposed that almost all psychologists could accept the following propositions as baselines:

Pervasive characteristics. Almost all characteristics of individual people correlate with age, education, intelligence, sex, and social class; and almost all characteristics of groups and organizations correlate with age, size, and wealth. An implication would be that every study should measure these variables and consider them.

Cognitive consonance. Simultaneously evoked cognitions (attitudes, beliefs, perceptions, and values) tend to become logically consistent (Festinger 1957; Heider 1958; Abelson et al. 1968). Corollary 1: Retrospection makes what has happened appear highly probable (Fischhoff 1980). Corollary 2: Social status, competence, control, and organizational attitudes tend toward congruence (Sampson, 1969; Payne and Pugh 1976). Corollary 3: Dissonant cognitions elicit subjective sensations such as feelings of inequity, and strong dissonance may trigger behaviors such as change initiatives or reduced participation (Walster et al. 1973). Corollary 4: Simultaneously evoked cognitions tend to polarize into one of two opposing clusters (Cartwright and Harary 1956). Corollary 5: People and social systems tend to resist change (Marx 1904; Lewin 1943).

Social propositions. Activities, interactions, and sentiments reinforce each other (Homans 1950). Corollary 1: People come to resemble their neighbors (Coleman, Katz, and Menzel 1966; Industrial Democracy in Europe International Research Group 1981). Corollary 2: Collectivities develop distinctive norms and shared beliefs (Roethlisberger and Dickson 1939; Seashore 1954; Beyer 1981). These propositions can also be viewed as corollaries of cognitive consonance.

Idea evaluation by other people inhibits idea generation (Maier 1963).

Participation in the implementation of new ideas makes the ideas more acceptable (Lewin 1943; Kelley and Thibaut 1954). Corollary 1: Participation in goal setting fosters the acceptance of goals (Maier 1963; Locke 1968; Vroom and Yetton 1973; Latham and Yukl 1975). Corollary 2: Participation in the design of changes reduces resistance to change (Coch and French 1948; Marrow, Bowers, and Seashore 1967; Lawler and Hackman 1969). Corollary 3: Opportunities to voice dissent make exit less likely (Hirschman 1970).

Reinforcement Propositions. Rewards make behaviors more likely, punishments make behaviors less likely (Thorndike 1911; Skinner 1953). These are tautologies, of course (Smedslund 1984), but so is Newton's $F = ma$. I include them to show that propositions need not convey information in order to facilitate consensus.

Immediate reinforcements have stronger impacts (Hull 1943).

Continuous reinforcements produce faster learning that is also unlearned more quickly, whereas intermittent reinforcements produce slower learning that is unlearned more slowly (Hull 1943; Estes 1957).

4.5 The 1990s

In the early 1990s, my investigations of knowledge-intensive firms drew me into a study of a very, very exceptional law firm, Wachtell, Lipton, Rosen, and Katz (Starbuck 1993b). This firm demonstrated that the advice management professors give to students really can produce outstanding results. The firm also amazed me not only for its extreme success both financially and legally but also for its idiosyncrasies. It differed significantly not only from a typical law firm but from other very successful law firms. This firm had a reputation for being able to win cases that other law firms regarded as unwinnable, and it won such cases by concocting novel legal strategies that set new precedents. This firm's revenue per lawyer was 88 percent higher than any other American law firm, and its profit per partner was 60 percent higher than any other firm. Its junior personnel expressed higher job satisfaction than those at any competing firm, and it promoted lawyers to partnership at nearly three times the average rate for other firms.

After I described this law firm at a conference, another speaker took me aside and explained in great seriousness that I should not be talking about this firm because it differed so greatly from other law firms. When he and a colleague had made a statistical study of law firms, he said, they had had to remove this idiosyncratic firm from their data because it had been distorting their calculations (Gilson and Mnookin 1989).

This advice quite astonished me, but it also reminded me vividly that I was working in a culture that eschews idiosyncrasy and celebrates averages. In order to report my observations about this law firm in a journal, I would have to explain why it is useful to study a single, unique case, and to do that, I would have to explain what is wrong with focusing exclusively of averages computed over large samples.

Therefore, I began my written report by explaining that studies that had searched for universally true propositions had yielded superficial or unimportant propositions or ones that people had accepted long before (Starbuck 1993b). Because people create new organizations to pursue goals that existing organizations are not achieving, there is pressure for the overall population of organizations to grow more diverse. To see how various properties foster success or survival, one needs to look at the differences among organizations. Furthermore, idiosyncrasy is likely to be transient. To become extremely profitable, a company has to exploit passing fads and fleeting opportunities; and to remain extremely profitable, a company has to resist forces that undermine its idiosyncrasies. Thus, it is useful to investigate not only what properties organizations have but also how they acquired these properties.

The prevalent research culture also assumed that an organization can be clearly defined and possesses identifiable properties. Researchers passed out questionnaires, averaged the responses, and interpreted these averages as organizational properties. However, I found that various participants in this law firm saw different organizations, and so did observers of it. This ambiguity arose not merely from the perceivers' different viewpoints but also from the law firm's complexity and internal inconsistencies. Insiders disagreed with each other about the firm's properties, and outsiders had difficulty understanding its properties. In fact, its unusual success was due in part to its competitors' inability to imitate it. If others could imitate it, they might be able to invent the kinds of legal tactics it had invented and they might be able to earn the high profits it was earning. However, there were several reasons competing firms could not imitate it, and one of these reasons was that they found its business practices mysterious.

Another prevalent belief among researchers was that successful organizations adapt to their environments. However, I observed that this exceptional firm was simultaneously a reflection of its environment and its historical era and an influential shaper of its environment and its era. Its founders had created the firm in reaction against conditions that existed at the time of its founding, and the firm's actions strongly influenced the structure of its industry—instigating changes in employment practices, in legal tactics, and in relations between lawyers and their clients. Arguments this firm had advanced in courts and cases it had won had altered indirectly the legally accepted definitions of business relationships and of employer–employee relations. In other words, the law firm had been an important component of its environment.

To me, this study had illustrated some of the limitations of studies of statistical averages and some of the advantages of studying exceptional cases. Although imitating an average may help a person or organization avoid abject failure, it cannot show how to attain great success. Although observing average behavior may help a person or organization to understand routinized adaptation, it cannot show

how to produce dramatic innovations, which have to be exceptional. Studies of dynamic mutual interactions between people or organizations and their environments tend to expose idiosyncrasies and to develop into studies of unusual or distinctive cases.

* * *

An article by Jeffreys and Berger (1992) showed me another way to improve on tests of statistical significance. Although replacing null hypotheses with naive models would be an improvement, any evaluation procedure that resembles a significance test has the disadvantage of treating truth as a binary variable. Traditional statistical tests assume that a hypothesis is either true or false. There are no degrees of uncertainty even though the conceptual foundations for the tests assume uncertainty. Jeffreys and Berger pointed out that likelihood ratios allow one to treat truth as a continuous variable. One computes the ratio:

$$\frac{\text{Probability (data if the focal model were true)}}{\text{Probability (data if the naive model were true)}}$$

If the focal model fits the data much better than the naive model does, the ratio will be substantially greater than one. One can then ask whether the ratio is large enough to justify the greater complexity associated with the focal model. However, there are no tables in the backs of statistics books to tell one the correct answers.

* * *

When John Mezias and I decided to study the accuracy of managers' perceptions, I worried about how many managers we would need in order to draw meaningful conclusions (Starbuck and Mezias 1996). I remembered that Schmidt (1971), Claudy (1972), and Dorans and Drasgow (1978) had run computer simulations that implied one needs hundreds of observations before the results of regression analysis would be more reliable than equally weighted independent variables. As well, Einhorn and Hogarth (1975) had compared regression with equally weighted independent variables. They had concluded: (*a*) Over wide ranges of sample sizes and numbers of independent variables, there is little difference between regression weights and equally weighted independent variables. (*b*) Equally weighted independent variables are more reliable than regression weights when samples are small, when multiple correlations are not high, or when

131

independent variables intercorrelate. With ten independent variables and multiple correlation coefficients below 0.5, samples might have to exceed 400 before regression weights become more reliable than equally weighted independent variables.

Thus, I knew that we would need data from hundreds of managers. However, I was worried because the studies above had assumed perfect Normal distributions. Mezias and I would not obtain data that would be perfectly Normal. One of our variables was binary and four of our variables were discrete and had skewed distributions. Thus, we would need more observations than indicated by calculations that assumed perfect Normal distributions.

I simulated our statistical problem by generating hypothetical data about how managers behave. My assumptions about the data we would obtain were partly based on data from 70 managers, but I had to augment those data by making assumptions that seemed realistic. I added large-enough errors to the dependent variable to make the multiple correlation coefficients approximate 0.4. Previous studies had produced much lower multiple correlations—between 0.1 and 0.2—so my simulations understate actual error in the dependent variable and also the sample sizes needed for reliable regression calculations. However, at the time, Mezias and I were optimistic that our study would yield higher correlations than the previous studies.

The key control condition in these simulation experiments was the sample size. The computer generated N hypothetical values of the independent and dependent variables, added errors to approximate managers' perceptual errors, computed regression coefficients with the sample, and saved the estimated coefficients. The regression calculations were ordinary least-squares regressions (OLS). Next, the computer generated a new sample of N observations, and calculated predicted values of the dependent variable by two methods:

1. The dependent variable equals the linear function estimated by OLS regression from the preceding sample.
2. The standardized value of the dependent variable equals K times the sum of the standardized values of the independent variables. I set the coefficient K equal to $1/Sqrt(5)$ so that the variance of the dependent variable would approximately equal the variance of the sum of the five independent variables.

The computer repeated this process fifty times for each sample size—20, 50, 100, 200, 500, and 1,000.

Because this process was a simulation rather than an analysis of empirical data, I knew the exact values of the coefficients used to generate data, and I could calculate the errors in the estimated effect sizes. The simulations showed that OLS regression had a significant likelihood of yielding large errors in estimated effect sizes for all the sample sizes below 1,000. If we obtained data from fewer than 1,000 managers, regression-based estimates about dependent variables would be less reliable than estimates we could make solely on a priori grounds.

Figure 4.4 compares the predictive accuracy of OLS regression with the predictive accuracy of equally weighted independent variables. The horizontal line at 1 represents the accuracy of predictions made with equally weighted independent variables, and the other three lines show the accuracy of predictions made with OLS regression— the average and 90 percent confidence limits. Whereas OLS sometimes produces more accurate predictions than do equally weighted variables, on average, OLS regression produced less accurate predictions for every sample size up to 1,000, so the average OLS prediction falls below the horizontal line at 1. For sample sizes much larger than those graphed, OLS regression would produce better predictions on average than equally weighted independent variables, but OLS

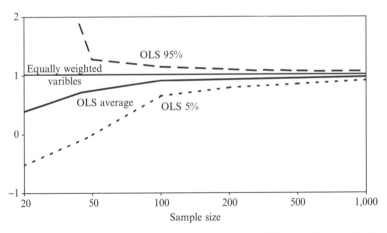

Figure 4.4 Ratio of fit with OLS regression to fit with equally weighted independent variables

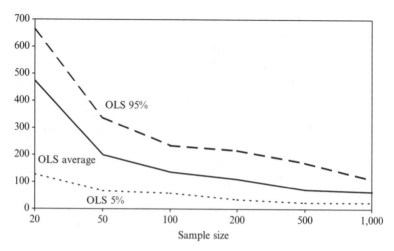

Figure 4.5 Maximum errors in effect sizes when estimated by OLS regression

regression does not produce greatly better predictions than equally weighted independent variables for even gigantic samples.

Figure 4.5 shows the distributions of the largest errors in regression coefficients estimated by OLS regression; these are the errors in the coefficients of standardized independent variables. For samples of 200, the largest errors averaged more than 108 percent and they remained at 62 percent even for samples of 1,000. The errors decrease as sample sizes increase but we would have needed a gigantic sample to be confident of our inferences about the importance of different independent variables.

I found the foregoing simulation results very disappointing and deeply disturbing. Although the forecasting literature said that the use of squared-error criteria results in poor forecasts, I had not understood how large the errors might be and, especially, I had not understood that OLS regression remains only a little better than equally weighted independent variables even for very, very large samples. Certainly, Mezias and I could not imagine a way to obtain data from more than 1,000 managers. If OLS regression were the only analytic tool available to us, we could make more accurate predictions if we did not obtain or analyze any data!

This was the point at which I developed an interest in alternatives to squared-error statistics. The essential problem with OLS regression is that the use of squared errors places great emphasis on outliers. Since a small sample contains just a few outliers, the peculiarities of specific outliers have great importance. Large samples have many outliers that tend to offset each other, so each outlier should exert weak influence and the peculiarities of specific outliers should have little importance. However, the sample sizes needed to achieve such balance are larger than the samples sizes that social scientists normally obtain (Kelley and Maxwell 2003).

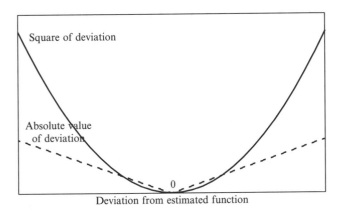

Figure 4.6 Influence of deviations on estimated functions

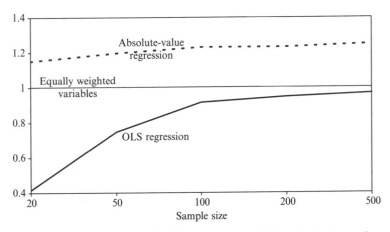

Figure 4.7 Ratios of fit with OLS regression and fit with absolute-value regression to fit with equally weighted independent variables

Looking for alternative methods, I ran across the idea of regression calculations that minimize sums of absolute values rather than sums of squares. Figure 4.6 illustrates the difference between absolute values and squared errors. Whereas squared errors rise rapidly as errors grow larger, the absolute values of errors rise linearly. As a result, extreme outliers do not dominate the coefficient estimates made by absolute-value regression. Therefore, I repeated my simulations while comparing OLS regression with absolute-value regression. As Figure 4.7 shows, on average, absolute-value regression yielded coefficient estimates that were more reliable than OLS, and also 15–25 percent more reliable than equally weighted independent variables. Although the improvement was not dramatic, I was thrilled to see that a way exists to make data gathering useful.

* * *

After listening to innumerable researchers' claim to have used multiple regression to verify the influence of independent variables on a dependent one, and reading innumerable journal articles that made such claims, I grew cynical about researchers' willingness to make 'convenient' assumptions instead of gathering data. In reaction, I formulated another rule for myself: 'Every regression equation should be a complete theory of the dependent variable.' This means to me that researchers should not assume that an unobserved variable has no effects on estimated regression coefficients. If a variable can affect the dependent variable, a researcher should observe it and include it in calculations. If a researcher would like to claim that a potentially relevant variable is so randomly distributed in the data that it has no effects on the coefficient estimates, the researcher should estimate the coefficients both with and without this variable and demonstrate that the coefficients are the same.

This rule is also relevant because so many researchers attempt to use regression calculations to demonstrate causality. Although regressions show correlation and not causality, researchers make assertions about causality when they state their 'theories' and they interpret regression coefficients as statements about the strengths of these causal relationships. Since these practices are so prevalent, trying to insist that regression equations actually approximate the stated causal theories seems like a rudimentary first step toward more relevant statistical analyses.

* * *

In 1994, Jacob Cohen, a highly esteemed psychometrician, published an article pointing out that psychologists were continuing to perform 'the ritual of null hypothesis significance testing' despite 'four decades of severe criticism'. He complained especially about 'the misinterpretation' that rejecting a null hypothesis 'affirms the theory that led to the test'. Cohen (1994) urged psychologists to make more use of graphic methods and to estimate confidence intervals for effect sizes. Generalization, he asserted, should be based on replication.

Cohen's article induced Albert E. Bartz to engage in conversations with a number of psychologists, and then to write a letter to the American Psychological Association (APA) in 1995. Author of several statistics textbooks, Bartz proposed that APA convene a task force or a conference to discuss the implications of Cohen's observations about statistical inference. APA staff added this issue to the next meeting of their Board of Scientific Affairs and put Bartz in contact with Frank Schmidt, another highly regarded psychometrician. Schmidt seconded Bartz's proposal, and in 1996, Schmidt published an article pointing out 'that reliance on statistical significance testing in the analysis and interpretation of research data has systematically retarded the growth of cumulative knowledge.... [W]e must abandon the statistical significance test.... [F]or analysis of data from individual studies, the appropriate statistics are point estimates of effect sizes and confidence intervals around these point estimates.... [F]or analysis of data from multiple studies, the appropriate method is meta-analysis' (Schmidt, 1996: 115).

These proposals caused a considerable stir. APA did appoint a task force to develop new recommendations about statistical inference, and symposia on significance testing took place at the annual meetings of both APA and the American Psychological Society (Abelson 1997; Estes 1997; Harris 1997; Hunter 1997; Scarr 1997; Shrout 1997). However, following a brief initial meeting, the APA task force announced that it 'does not support any action that could be interpreted as banning the use of null hypothesis significance testing or p values' (Task Force on Statistical Significance 1996). They did, however, say that they planned to investigate several areas in which psychological researchers could improve methodology. The final report of the task force discussed a wide range of methodological issues, but the advice did include 'always present effect sizes' and 'Interval estimates should be given for any effect sizes' (Wilkinson and Task Force 1999).

* * *

In 1995, Steve Kerr, a manager with academic interests, proposed to Rick Mowday, then the president of the Academy of Management, that the Academy should undertake activities similar to those of an organization called the Marketing Science Institute (MSI). Mowday did not act on Kerr's proposal, but he passed the proposal to me when I became the Academy's president in 1997. MSI's achievements impressed me greatly.

In existence since 1961, MSI encourages academic research in marketing that relates to contemporary managerial problems and has potential for application. During recent years, MSI has had more than sixty member companies and its influence in the field of marketing has been remarkable. Over a recent ten-year period, projects that MSI sponsored won every award for outstanding research in marketing and they comprised 60 percent of the articles in the *Journal of Marketing* and the *Journal of Marketing Research*. During 2003, MSI-sponsored projects won two awards for research that had had significant impacts over long periods, and won one of the two awards for the best research published during 2003. Probably more importantly, MSI has sponsored two-way dialogues between managers and researchers. MSI's premise is that theory and practice can and should reinforce each other: Good theory can improve practice, and good practice can lead to good theory. Of course, the auxiliary verb 'can' is essential because mutual benefits are far from automatic.

Every other year, MSI's member companies identify research priorities, which MSI then circulates to 2,000 academic researchers around the world. Academic researchers propose projects, and thirty to thirty-five new projects begin each year, so about ninety projects are underway at any time. Because the reports from projects tend to be technical and academic, MSI hires professional business writers to restate the reports as executive summaries that draw out implications for practice. MSI's reports go to around 2,000 researchers and 2,000 managers. Member-only conferences and implementation workshops also discuss research findings and develop their practical implications. A typical conference involves forty managers and twenty researchers and emphasizes dialogue among the participants.

The benefits of MSI sponsorship are mainly conceptual and facilitative. Sponsored projects receive only modest financial support. MSI's activities produce better research mainly by helping researchers to ask better questions, to make better analyses of questions before they gather data, to obtain better data, and to make better analyses of the implications of research findings. Of course, not every question that companies find interesting is important from a theoretical point of view, but companies ask questions because the answers are not obvious to them. This implies that the questions touch on core issues that challenge accepted beliefs. Discussions between researchers and managers about research designs help to clarify what issues can be investigated from a practical viewpoint. The support of participating companies can improve the quality of data by raising response rates, by phrasing questions more intelligibly, and by motivating respondents to respond sincerely. Discussions between researchers and managers about research findings can both help researchers to understand the value and limitations of their work and help them to pose better questions in the future.

My own experience suggests that the goals of nearly all academic management researchers can be rendered compatible with the goals of companies that serve as research sites. The main reason is that the issues that academic researchers want to investigate are nearly irrelevant from the companies' viewpoint and the issues that companies want to investigate are nearly irrelevant from the viewpoint of academic researchers. For example, companies usually focus on immediate, short-term issues that change constantly whereas researchers are primarily interested in long-term issues that evolve slowly. Such mutual irrelevance makes it possible to construct research designs that satisfy the needs of both. Researchers can help companies to find answers they seek while also asking questions that interest the researchers themselves, and conversely, companies can help researchers to find answers they seek while also getting answers that interest the companies. Mutual compatibility is especially likely when researchers want to study prevalent, general human behavior because such topics can be investigated in diverse settings. However, it does require a bit of imagination and flexibility to develop research plans that frame researchers' questions within the applied perspectives of companies. Both researchers and companies must be willing to give something to get something.

For example, John Mezias and I (2003) wanted realistic data about the accuracy of managers' perceptions. Because our interest in this topic arose from questions about the effectiveness of managers' strategizing, we thought we wanted to study managers' perceptions of the variables in theories about strategies. However, we had found that managers do not think in terms of the variables in theories about strategies and that it is difficult even to discuss such variables with managers. As a result, we were dissatisfied with our first study of this topic and we were looking for a way to obtain better data.

We approached a senior corporate manager in one of the world's largest companies, and after eight months of negotiations, we gained the company's support for our project. The senior corporate manager said that the company's top priority was quality improvement and we could gather data only if the data would tell the company how it was doing in that domain. Had we been designing a study without concern for its relevance to anyone else, we would not have chosen quality improvement as the target subject. But managers' do have perceptions in this domain and the company was spending a lot of resources trying to measure quality, so we would have access to good measures of 'objective reality' to compare with the managers' perceptions. Furthermore, one deficiency of our earlier research had been uncertainty about the degrees to which our respondents regarded our questions as pertinent.

Personnel in each of four large divisions helped us to design questionnaires that suited the managers in their divisions. We also felt confident that the variables we were studying were relevant and important to our respondents. Many managers had attended training courses about quality improvement, each division had a department that focused on quality improvement, and all managers were receiving quality measures frequently. Three-quarters of the managers who filled out our questionnaires told us that they expected to receive large increases in their personal rewards if their divisions achieved higher quality. Therefore, by focusing our questions on quality improvement, we made it significantly more likely that our respondents understood our questions and regarded our questions as pertinent.

Although we had studied quality improvement because it had been the highest priority of the corporate managers, it was no longer the highest priority one year later when we sought follow-up data. The senior corporate manager who had helped us was attending to other projects, and his assistant who had helped us had moved to a different job. We still wanted data about the accuracy of managers' perceptions, and to maintain consistency with our previous work, we wanted data about quality improvement, but the company had developed new interests.

There are obvious limitations to research funded by business firms and approved by managers. However, much academic research is wasting talent and opportunities by attempting to answer poorly phrased questions with very low-quality data. Therefore, with help from several people, I spent more than two years trying to start a research institute resembling MSI and devoted to management research. Many senior scholars were willing to contribute time to such an enterprise and a large number of senior managers were willing to ask their companies to pay annual dues for such a purpose. The managers did not express interest in sponsoring research as such, but they were willing to sponsor research as a way to influence business education. Managers also saw seminars and two-way conversations with researchers as effective ways to enhance the professional development of themselves and their colleagues. I became convinced that a research institute could attract forty to sixty companies, but starting it would require around US$2,000,000, which I did not find.

5

The Production of Knowledge

'Knowledge and error flow from the same mental sources, only the result distinguishes the two.'

—Ernst Mach (1905; p. 116 in the 1987 reprint)

Although it is easy to see why social scientists appreciate a system that allows large numbers of them to appear to be highly productive, tens of thousands of quite intelligent researchers are spending their time producing little or nothing of lasting value. Because the utilitarian value of their research is so low, their social environment pays little attention to their research and regards social scientists with amused indulgence. Social science research that sets higher standards for the dependability of its findings would have more value for society and would bring greater respect to researchers themselves.

This chapter proposes some research tactics that, I believe, would improve research results. These tactics would certainly not solve all problems, but they can weed out some noise and yield more robust knowledge that is less dependent on who did the research. The next two sections advocate that researchers should both challenge their own thinking by disrupting their preconceptions and try to demonstrate the validity of their knowledge by observing natural experiments and by displacing situations from equilibria. The third section focuses on statistical methods that emphasize the production of dependable, robust knowledge. Finally, recognizing that knowledge is essentially human and social, the last section urges researchers to strive to create consensus about what they know. Before knowledge can accumulate, people must agree that they want knowledge to accumulate. Such agreement confronts barriers such as vested interests and widespread practices.

Because the problems I am trying to address arise from doing what seems natural or conventional, most of my proposed tactics may seem unnatural or unconventional. In my experience, these perceptions fade as the tactics become more familiar and one experiences the advantages of using them.

5.1 Disturbing Oneself

'Arguments are to be avoided; they are always vulgar and often convincing.'

—Oscar Wilde, *The Importance of Being Earnest* (Act II, 1895)

The comfort of logical consistency is so intrinsic to human experience that there may be no way to persuade a human mind that it is desirable to be illogical. However, logic creates prisons that blind researchers and limit their discoveries. By challenging their explicit assumptions and the validity of their inferences, researchers can gain perspective on the situations they are studying and discover implicit assumptions of which they were unaware.

Perhaps the gentlest disturbance one can give to one's thinking is linguistic, a change of vocabulary or grammar. There is no doubt that language affects thought. Some linguistic changes have more profound effects than do others, of course. One of the more profound changes that I have experienced came after I adopted a policy of using active verbs and avoiding passive verbs and forms of 'to be'. This policy, adopted mainly to make my writing clearer and more persuasive, subtly and progressively altered my ways of thinking. I became dissatisfied with the kinds of theories I had earlier deemed adequate, and in particular, I began to pay much more attention to causal processes. A less profound change occurred after I noticed that researchers often use the definite article 'the' where an indefinite article would be accurate. For example, researchers often say 'the organization' where they are actually discussing numerous organizations having diverse properties; by saying 'the organization', researchers construct homogeneity in heterogeneous phenomena by speaking as if all organizations are alike. After

I began to watch for such usages, I saw more dispersion in phenomena, both at one time and over time; and I became more aware of ways in which researchers fabricate homogeneity artificially, possibly misleading themselves and certainly misleading their readers.

Triangulation—investigating a situation with more than one type of data—offers another gentle way to disturb one's thinking. For example, Sutton and Rafaeli (1988) examined relationships between sales volume and the emotions that employees display to customers. A chain of convenience stores attempted to gain a competitive advantage by persuading employees to smile and act friendly toward customers. Sutton and Rafaeli attempted to assess the results by surreptitiously observing employees' behavior. The behaviors the company had thought desirable correlated negatively with store sales. Where employees were smiling, stores had lower sales; where employees were not friendly, stores had higher sales. Therefore, Sutton and Rafaeli approached this topic through an alternative methodology. They gathered qualitative data through interviews and through working in stores themselves. These new data indicated that store sales reflected employees' workloads as determined by the flows of customers through stores: stores with high sales had many customers and employees had no time to exchange pleasantries with customers. Thus, surprising findings from statistical analyses became understandable through direct observation; the researchers broke free of their initial premises by coming at the situation from a different direction.

The term 'triangulation' implies that one is looking at the same object from two or more perspectives, but the object itself may change when one changes perspective (Lewis and Grimes 1999). Hence, triangulation may be like the legendary blind men studying not an elephant but six different animals. In particular, triangulation always seems to involve different levels of analysis—for instance, individual employees talking to individual customers, versus sales by many stores over several months and observations about many employees. Aggregation or disaggregation can have dramatic implications. An average of many instances may describe very few of them, possibly none. A correlation across a population may occur in none of the subpopulations. A true statement about a population may be false for every member of the population.

All dissents and warnings have some validity.
Collaborators who disagree are both right.
All causal arrows have two heads.
The converse of every proposition is equally valid.

To disturb one's brain more abruptly, one can use logic to counteract logic. One can induce one's brain to extrapolate the logical consequences of various hypothetical conjectures. If these conjectures deny one's current perceptions, their logical consequences can disclose the limitations of those perceptions. One can also juxtapose two lines of reasoning that contradict each other. The resulting dilemmas can disclose the limitations of one's reasoning.

One can use such contradictions either as an individual or as a member of a social unit. Two social forms of contradiction are generally useful. The proposition that 'all dissents and warnings have some validity' offers a reminder that people perceive different phenomena and hold different values (Starbuck 1996). Similarly, 'collaborators who disagree are both right' can induce one to view a situation from an alternative perspective. Both propositions motivate one to see larger pictures, to take account of additional causal processes, to recognize the legitimacy of different goals, or to examine other sources of information.

One can also apply two of these propositions as an individual—'all causal arrows have two heads' and 'the converse of every proposition is equally valid.' The first of these encourages one to look for longer-run feedback paths that may be setting the slow-changing context for shorter-run causal links. The second proposition offers a reminder that truths are rarely clear-cut and situations are almost always more complex than one has yet acknowledged.

I phrase these propositions in quite absolute terms in order to force my brain to contemplate what it has been ignoring, to reconsider what it has been assuming. Of course, there must be situations in which dissents are invalid and there must be propositions that lack valid converses. However, if I were to say 'some dissents and warnings have some validity', it would be entirely too easy for me to deny the validity of dissents and warnings. I need to compel myself to give full consideration to the possible validity of dissents and warnings, so I demand that I search for all possible evidence of validity. Likewise, if I were to say 'the converses of some propositions are equally valid,' I would find it entirely too easy to deny the validity of converse propositions. As I see it, my mind creates blinders that block out new, different, or inconsistent perceptions, so I must use extreme measures to tear away these blinders.

One can view the propositions that 'collaborators who disagree are both right' and 'the converse of every proposition is equally valid' as examples of dialectical thinking, which is the most generally useful way to use logic to expand one's perceptions. In dialectical thinking, one starts with a proposition (a thesis), such as 'A causes B' or 'X is good'. One then formulates a contradictory proposition (an antithesis), such as 'B causes A' or 'X is bad'. Finally, one tries to integrate (synthesize) both propositions into a single perspective, such as 'A and B influence each other' or 'X has both good and bad consequences'.

In my experience, dialectical thinking nearly always yields valid insights about situations. I explain this with the idea that we humans are rather simple creatures who live in rather complex worlds. We tend to view our worlds in clear, simple terms that are easy for us to understand. But in so doing, we oversimplify our worlds, neglect their ambiguities, and overlook their nuances. Dialectical thinking helps us to overcome our limitations to a small degree (Starbuck 1988).

Collaborative research can stimulate and support dialectic thinking. When two or more researchers start from different premises and advocate different theories, they expose their collaborators to alternative interpretations. Collaboration then encourages the researchers to reconcile their disparate theories, and they tend to do this by developing more holistic theories. I reported in the preceding chapter how a dispute with Hedberg stimulated collaboration between us and eventually persuaded both of us that we had initially been partly right and partly wrong (Starbuck 1989). Another example is afforded by a controversy between Latham and Erez, who had obtained quite different results from their experiments. After enlisting Locke as a mediator, Latham and Erez ran four experiments to sort out the issues (Latham, Erez, and Locke 1988). They discovered that the differences between their prior experiments had been due not to their overt experimental controls but to the ways each had given instructions to their experimental subjects. Locke (Latham, Erez, and Locke 1988: 769) remarked:

[W]hat struck me the most was the number of differences in procedure and design that can occur when two people are allegedly studying the same phenomenon. In this case there were at least nine differences in the procedures or designs of the [prior] Erez and Latham studies. Some of these were quite subtle (e.g. self-efficacy instructions). Many were not evident from reading the printed version of the studies (e.g. differences between tell and tell-and-sell instructions; telling subjects to reject disliked goals). If such differences occurred in these studies, one can assume that they also must occur in studies of other phenomena.

Dialectic thinking often occurs socially during the development of social science theories, as researchers react to unsatisfactory propositions by integrating them with their contradictions. For example, in the USA and much of Europe during the late nineteenth century, scientific psychology was a science of perception that relied on introspective evidence (Starbuck 2000). Shortly after 1900, a behaviorist revolution challenged the existing methods. Behaviorists argued that introspection produces very unreliable data and that cognitive processes are consequences of behavior rather than causes of it. Although debate continued during the 1930s and 1940s, psychological research focused on behaviors and largely ignored cognition. In one classic debate, Tolman (1948) argued that his experimental evidence showed that some rats developed cognitive maps of their environments that enabled them to innovate effectively. However, Guthrie and Horton (1946: 7) argued that speculation about thought processes was unnecessary to explain the behaviors of cats: 'We do not at all deny that the cat undoubtedly has experience analogous to ours. But it appears to us highly desirable to find an adequate description of the cat's behavior without recourse to such conscious experience.'

Nevertheless, psychologists found it difficult to extrapolate behavioral studies of simple animals to people and they grew ready for a new approach (Chomsky 1959). In the 1950s, Newell, Simon, and others began to use computer programs as models of cognitive processes (Newell and Simon 1956; Newell, Shaw, and Simon 1958). This initiated a revitalized interest in cognition. Starting in the 1970s, cognitive studies began to dominate the flagship journals and the doctoral dissertations in psychology. During the late 1960s, psychologists cited behaviorist studies about twice as often as cognitive studies (Robins, Gosling, and Craik 1998). By the mid-1990s, psychologists were citing cognitive studies five times as often as behaviorist studies.

However, this shift from behaviorist to cognitive represents incomplete dialectic thinking as yet, for researchers have not integrated behavior and cognition into an encompassing framework that shows how they represent alternative aspects of phenomena. Cognitive theories can explain phenomena that behaviorist theories cannot; but as well, behaviorist theories can explain phenomena that cognitive theories cannot (Starbuck 2000; Starbuck and Hedberg 2001). Only a few of the most radical behaviorists have denied that cognition sometimes guides human behavior, but the influence of cognition on behavior has to be loose or highly variable and the influence of behavior on cognition is often strong.

More complete dialectic thinking has occurred in theories about leadership (Webster and Starbuck 1988). During the early part of the twentieth century, many writers and managers held that successful organizations require firm leaders and obedient subordinates. Psychologists and managers viewed leadership as a stable characteristic of individuals, that is, some fortunate people have inherent leadership traits whereas others lack them. This orthodoxy attracted contradictory propositions: Weber (1947) noted that some organizations depersonalize leadership, and that subordinates sometimes judge leaders to be illegitimate. The Hawthorne studies argued that friendly supervision increases subordinates' productivity (Roethlisberger and Dickson, 1939; Mayo, 1946). Barnard (1937) asserted that authority originates in subordinates rather than in superiors.

By mid century, psychologists were proposing ways to integrate these differing views. Coch and French (1948) and Lewin (1953) spoke of democratic leadership. Bales (1953), Cartwright and Zander (1953), and Gibb (1954) analyzed leadership as an activity shared by several group members. Bales (1953) distinguished leaders' social roles from their task roles. Cattell and Stice (1954) and Stogdill (1948) considered the distinctive personality attributes of different kinds of leaders. By the late 1950s, the Ohio State studies had factored leadership into two dimensions—initiating structure and consideration (Fleishman, Harris, and Burtt 1955; Stogdill and Coons 1957). Initiating structure corresponds closely to the leadership concepts of 1910, and consideration corresponds to the challenges to those concepts. Thus, views that psychologists had originally seen as mutually contradictory gradually became independent dimensions of multiple and complex phenomena.

When different ideas are both valid, there must be a way to integrate the ideas into an encompassing framework that shows how the ideas can be consistent. Discovering such encompassing frameworks is the main purpose of dialectical thinking. Nevertheless, it is important that we do not integrate contrasting intellectual perspectives too rapidly, for we need contrasts as much as we need consistency. Contrasts help us to clarify concepts and warn us to avoid integrating concepts too easily. Juxtaposition and specialization foster new theories. In the long run, we make progress by framing issues as conflicts and then convincing ourselves gradually that the conflicts do not exist.

Yet another way to disturb oneself is to investigate extreme cases—situations or behaviors that appear to be extremely different from average situations or behaviors. Because the phenomena one observes most often strongly influence one's expectations, extreme cases challenge one's understanding. Extreme cases can expose overlooked causal factors and make one aware of the complexity of phenomena. In particular, people, organizations, and social systems develop symbiotically with their environments, so one needs to sensitize oneself to the feedback paths by which systems interact. Extreme cases can also discourage overgeneralization and foster appreciation for individuality and variety. All people, all organizations, all social systems are partly unique, so one needs to sensitize oneself to the differences among things as well as their similarities.

One challenge for studies of extreme cases is to sort out what makes the cases extreme. When the past influences the future, systems can develop differentiation merely because they have had different experiences (Denrell 2004). The processes that cause extreme events may not be extreme and they may be normal. In one series of studies, Hedberg, Nystrom, and I examined organizations that appeared to be confronting serious crises (Starbuck 1989). When we began these studies we thought we were looking for abnormalities, but our studies revealed that abnormality had been an error in our prior beliefs; nearly all organizations confront crises that threaten their existence at one time or another. Although crises put many organizations out of business, some organizations confront crises more than once. Thus, serious crises are not actually rare, although they do constitute extreme situations in comparison with organizations' normal challenges. These extreme situations emerge from normal developmental processes in organizations and in their environments. Perrow (1984) also argued that extreme situations—serious industrial accidents—may arise from normal processes, and that normal processes make accidents very likely to occur sooner or later. Based on reviews of major accidents in several industries, Perrow inferred that complex systems with tight couplings between their components have multitude ways to fail. Furthermore, such systems are so difficult to control that efforts to prevent accidents may instead produce accidents.

Studies of exceptional performance are inevitably concerned with extreme cases, and to understand the requirements of exceptional performance, one must study extreme cases, not averages. Furthermore, if one is concerned with exceptional performance by organizations, it seems that one has to anticipate the need for complex explanations. One reason for complexity is that organizations that perform exceptionally well do so by exploiting properties of their environments. This exploitation alters the environments, so the environments reflect the organizations' presence, and the organizations develop interdependently with their environments. Furthermore, complexity impedes imitation. If one could explain an organization's exceptional performance simply, the organization would acquire effective competitors and it would no longer perform exceptionally well.

Some of these issues are illustrated by my study of an exceptional law firm, Wachtell, Lipton, Rosen, and Katz (Starbuck 1993*b*). Two studies of law firms had produced similar findings about average statistics. Both Gilson and Mnookin (1989) and Samuelson and Jaffe (1990) inferred that the main determinant of profitability is 'leverage', which is the ratio of nonpartner associate lawyers to partners. Calculating across many law firms, they found that higher profit per partner correlated with higher leverage. This is the case because most law firms charge clients hourly rates that greatly exceed the wages they pay to associate lawyers, and the partners pocket the difference. However, Wachtell's leverage was significantly lower than that at any other major law firm, it compensated its associates more highly than did other firms, and when it charged clients by the hour, its rates were proportional to the wages of the lawyers who worked on those specific cases. Thus, Wachtell deviated explicitly from the pattern that supposedly determined profitability, yet Wachtell was the most profitable corporate law firm in the USA.

Indeed, Wachtell deviated significantly not only from a typical corporate law firm but also from other high-performing corporate law firms. Of course, Wachtell had properties that were shared by all other law firms and properties that were shared by some other law firms. However, Wachtell also had unique properties that other law firms could imitate but did not and unique properties that other law firms could not imitate. The latter properties are crucial because, to be exceptional, an organization must have a unique combination of properties. Either some of its properties must be very difficult or impossible for other organizations to acquire, or the exceptional organization has an ability to combine properties that other organizations find incompatible. If competing firms could readily imitate the properties of Wachtell and their leaders had the same goals as Wachtell's leaders, then Wachtell would no longer be exceptional. But Wachtell had properties that outsiders had difficulty understanding. Some of Wachtell's distinctive properties came from its founders and the societal context in which they founded the firm, and other distinctive properties developed as the firm's leaders reacted to various experiences. Thus, Wachtell has reflected its environment and its historical era, and it has also influenced its environment and its era.

I see disturbing oneself as a way to extend the utility of the human brain as a research tool. It affords a way to discover one's implicit assumptions and to gain different, and hopefully better, perceptions of the situations one is studying. However, effective research also requires studying the right situations, phenomena that are revealing. The next section discusses ways to disturb one's environment.

5.2 Disturbing One's Environment

Social systems are very capable of creating misleading impressions of their capabilities and limitations. They rarely violate critical constraints, and indeed, they are unlikely even to come close to violating them. They also remain close to equilibrium in almost all dimensions nearly all the time, so they do not exhibit the full range of behaviors of which they are capable. Studies of the existing social systems tend to ignore dynamics and to overlook causal factors than can influence dynamics. They leave nearly all degrees of freedom unexplored, and they do not show what could happen in abnormal circumstances. They give little information about forces that no one dares to challenge, yet these can be very important forces—such as constraints that a system dare not violate, or power so great that everyone respects it. They emphasize equilibria, de-emphasize reorientations, and may not show how equilibrating processes work. Studies of social systems in tranquil states highlight properties that many social systems share, but generality brings with it superficiality, as the most universal properties and relations are ones that serve ceremonial functions having weak utility.

151

To appreciate the full ranges of potential behaviors, one needs to see how social systems operate in unusual circumstances. 'Natural experiments' are situations in which normal behavior patterns have been or are being interrupted (Starbuck 1976). These natural experiments occur when exogenous events displace social systems from their normal equilibria. As a result, one can see some of systems' adaptive and reactive capabilities, which opens the possibility of discovering why equilibria exist.

Alan Meyer's study of hospitals provides an excellent example. Meyer had gathered data about some hospitals and was writing his analysis when insurance companies announced a dramatic increase in their premiums for doctors (Meyer 1982a, 1982b). The doctors decided to protest by going on strike, and Meyer decided to return to the hospitals and observe the hospitals' reactions to this strike. Some hospitals had predicted that a strike might occur and had developed contingency plans; others had not. Some hospitals remained profitable throughout the strike and the strike showed them how to be more profitable than before; others lost money during the strike. Meyer's predictions about how the hospitals would respond, based on his prior observations, proved incorrect. He had based his predictions on the hospitals' structures and routines, but hospitals' shared ideologies correlated distinctly more strongly with their reactions to the strike than did their structures or routines. A strong correlate of hospitals' responses was whether top managers had described their organizations as being like machines or like organisms when Meyer had interviewed them earlier.

Meyer observed what he called a 'jolt'—a temporary disruption of normal behaviors. Another jolt occurred at NASA when the Challenger space shuttle blew up (Starbuck and Milliken 1988). In this instance, a launch with very low ambient temperature put a spotlight on incremental processes that had received too little attention. Incremental improvements, intended to make the solid rocket boosters lighter and more powerful, had transformed a possibly safe design into an unworkable one. Then, gradual acclimatization to the damage to O-rings had blinded some managers to the significance of this damage and had caused them to misinterpret it as a sign that the rockets were robust rather than dangerous. The Challenger disaster also showed that behavior NASA regarded as normal, its claim that its space flights were routine, made absurd assumptions about the reliability of their technology and about astronauts' abilities to overcome deficiencies in hardware.

Jolts somewhat resemble the impulse functions or step functions that electronic engineers use to see inside 'black boxes'. One cannot gain a thorough understanding of a circuit by watching its response to a steady, unchanging input; but one can gain a substantially greater understanding of a circuit by watching its response to abrupt impulses or sudden changes in the input level. However, there is a significant difference between the study of electronic circuits and social systems. Electronic engineers assume that the contents of their black boxes remain constant, whereas jolts change both the behaviors that social systems exhibit and the social systems' future characteristics. For example, jolts can redistribute resources among a group of competitors, or jolts can teach people new skills and give them new perceptions.

Jolts create opportunities for change. They provide opportunities for some organizations to gain first-mover advantages or to escape from declining environments. They disrupt routines, energize members, and mobilize advocates. 'Garbage can' decision-making occurs, as decision-making situations elicit additional issues and actions that people would like to push as solutions (Cohen, March, and Olsen 1972). From a researcher's perspective, jolts constitute natural experiments that reveal obscure or inactive properties. Jolts also expose differences among overtly similar leaders, belief systems, and organizations, and they reveal hidden boundary conditions. Jolts teach lessons about system dynamics; they activate processes that seek to restore prior equilibria and to establish new equilibria; they show the symbiotic interactions between organizations and their environments.

Although natural experiments are certainly useful sources of information, they do not test theories' predictive efficacy. Nearly all analyses of natural experiments are retrospective, and because researchers can make retrospective theories consistent with the prominent stylized facts, such theories appear to perform adequately. At best, retrospective analyses of natural experiments encourage researchers to add contingencies to their theories. To expose theories' inadequacies more clearly, researchers must try to derive predictions from their theories and verify that what happens corresponds closely to what they predicted. In addition, the determinants of natural experiments have nothing to do with their usefulness as tests of theory, whereas significant theoretical progress depends on crucial experiments that rule out unproductive lines of thought. Therefore, to make significant scientific progress, researchers must sooner-or-later attempt to conduct crucial experiments and to validate their theories predictively.

Experimentation with people who are living real lives has long been a challenge for social scientists. Even researchers are not interested in being the subjects of research if their participation could threaten their livelihoods or career prospects (Riecken and Boruch 1974; Rivlin and Timpane 1975; Campbell and Russo 1998). Especially where outcomes may harm or benefit large numbers of people, this limits the feasible experiments to those that appear to offer benefits without risk, and it means that subjects are not randomized because they select themselves into treatments.

However, the interactions between researchers and their potential subjects can themselves be quite valuable. For one thing, potential subjects are very likely to withhold their participation until they receive credible predictions about outcomes. This negotiation not only forces researchers to make predictions but to do so using theories that potential subjects find plausible. This constitutes a weak verification that the predictive theories are not too implausible and that researchers have substantiation for their predictions. For another thing, potential subjects are very likely to evaluate predicted outcomes according to different criteria than researchers do. Indeed, researchers sometimes characterize themselves as acting purely objectively without being influenced by their personal values. Everyone benefits when potential subjects compel researchers to take note of their personal values and how these values influence research.

That said, however, it has been my experience that the goals of researchers are often uncorrelated with the goals of potential subjects. One needs to approach a situation without a strong commitment to a specific experimental design and with a range of possibilities in mind. Then, one needs to investigate the desires of the potential subjects, the objective being to design experiments that fulfill some of the desires of the potential subjects while also meeting research goals. Although the negotiations can be lengthy, even tortuous, the results can be higher quality data bearing more directly on significant issues.

King (1974) reported a field experiment with job design that illustrates the potential of experimental intervention. The experiment took place in four plants operated by one company. Plants 1 and 2 experimented with 'job enlargement' in which machine crews both set up their machines and inspected their own finished work. The other two plants, 3 and 4, experimented with 'job rotation' in which workers moved from one task to another at scheduled intervals. Thus, the experiment appeared to be comparing the results of job enlargement with those of job rotation. However, there was also another difference between plants. When the director of manufacturing explained the reasons for the experiment to the four plant managers, he gave different explanations. He told the managers of plants 1 and 3 that past research implied that the job changes would raise productivity, and he told the managers of plants 2 and 4 that past research implied that the job changes would not affect productivity but would improve 'industrial relations'. As it turned out, where the plant managers had been told to expect higher productivity, productivity was 6 percent higher over the ensuing twelve months; and where the plant managers had been told to expect better industrial relations, absenteeism was 12 percent lower over the ensuing twelve months. Productivity at the two job-enlargement plants was only 0.4 percent higher than at the two job-rotation plants, and absenteeism at the two job-enlargement plants differed by less than 1 percent from that at the two job-rotation plants. Thus, the changes in workers' actual activities had tiny effects, whereas the differences in the plant managers' expectations seemingly had much larger effects.

A willingness to help other people solve their problems also contributes, I believe, to general societal support for research. I have lived and been employed for periods from several months to several years in seven countries, I have visited academic institutions in eight other countries for briefer periods; and I have participated in academic meetings in another nine countries. I think I have seen loose correlations between academics' efforts to contribute to their societies, the quality of academic research, and the willingness of their societies to support academic research. I have surmised that where citizens perceive their universities to be contributing to their economic and social welfare, academic wages tend to be higher and research funds more available, and researchers seem to be generally more committed to doing research. By contrast, where citizens perceive their universities as arcane enclaves, academic wages tend to be lower and research funds scarcer, and researchers seem to be generally less committed to doing research. If my surmise is right, it is not only academics who are passing judgment on the value of academic research.

5.3 Emphasizing Statistical Robustness and Dependability

The preceding sections presented ideas that apply to both quantitative and nonquantitative research, and this section focuses on statistical methods. Statistical methods deserve special attention because they have generated so much noise.

Both methods for classifying data and inferences drawn from data depend on the completeness of the data themselves. If the data omit an important variable, no computation technique can overcome this omission. Social scientists often make the heroic assumption that omitted variables do not distort inferences, but such assumptions often seem implausible in the absence of evidence. Therefore, it makes sense for the consumers of research to demand that a regression equation should represent a complete theory of the dependent variable in the sense that every variable that may have an important influence on the dependent variable appears in the regression equation.

One high priority should be ending the almost universal misuse of tests of statistical significance tests. However, history shows that doing this is far from easy. People began pointing out the deficiencies of significance tests in the 1950s, and the opponents of significance tests have included many of the most respected methodologists (Falk and Greenbaum 1995). Thus, actually ending this practice seems to be a very remote possibility, and it seems more fruitful to whittle away at some of significance tests' undesirable properties—specifically, drawing binary inferences, drawing partial-derivative inferences about components of models, using incredible point null hypotheses, and relying strongly on the accuracy of the Normal distribution.

5.3.1 Likelihood Ratios and Naive Hypotheses

Traditional significance tests assume that a hypothesis is either utterly true or utterly false, even though the underlying statistical logic says that observations entail random errors. If uncertainty attaches to data, uncertainty must also accompany inferences from the data. Furthermore, calculations with a model depend on the entire model, not on individual components of it, so inferences about the plausibility of a model should be inferences about the entire model. Likelihood ratios deal with such matters more sensibly than do significance tests (Jeffreys and Berger 1992). One calculates a ratio such as

$$\frac{\text{Probability(data if model A were true)}}{\text{Probability(data if model B were true)}}$$

If the two models fit the data equally well, the ratio will be one. If model A fits the data much better than model B does, the ratio will be substantially greater than one. One is making a judgment not about truth but about the relative effectiveness of two models, treating each as a complete model.

Admittedly, one can still engage in partial-derivative thinking by adding or subtracting elements of a model. For example,

$$\frac{\text{Probability (data if model A(omitting variable X) were true)}}{\text{Probability(data if model A were true)}}$$

This seems an inevitable extrapolation of the current practice of trying to isolate the influence of individual variables. However, each such calculation has an attached consumer-warning label reminding researchers and their audiences that only a single modification of the model is being considered.

Replacing null hypotheses with naive hypotheses would set higher standards for claims about the importance of inferences (Starbuck 1994). Instead of claiming that one's theory is better than an utterly implausible set of assumptions, one can attempt to claim that the theory is better than assumptions that require no causal insight. These naive assumptions have many possible forms, such as tomorrow will be the same as today, or changes will follow linear trends, or the numbers of observations in various categories are unrelated to the actual meaning of the categories. The possibility of using different naive hypotheses is yet another way to get away from binary judgments about truth, because in most situations, it makes sense to consider more than one naive hypothesis.

5.3.2 Effect Sizes and Meta-Analysis

Another way to back away from binary judgments about truth is to talk about effect sizes (Kirk 1996; Nix and Barnette 1998). Although researchers routinely use t-values as measures of the influence of independent variables, contingencies, or control conditions on a dependent variable, t-values are not actually comparable measures of influence because they do not allow for the variation exhibited by each factor. For example, if one estimates the coefficients in the equation

$$Z = A^*X + B^*Y$$

the *t*-values for *A* and *B* do not take account of the possibility that *X* may vary much more than does *Y*. Standardized regression coefficients might provide better estimates of the influence of *X* and *Y*, as they estimate the amount of change in *Z* that would occur if *X* changes by one standard deviation versus the amount of change in *Z* that would occur if *Y* changes by one standard deviation. Standardized regression coefficients make sense, however, only if *X* and *Y* are actually random variables, e.g. randomly sampled from a large population.

It is quite easy to find published studies that have reported practically trivial differences that are statistically significant or practically important differences that are not statistically significant. Webster and I (1988) found that large sample studies and small sample studies obtain very similar distributions of correlations, but the small sample studies produce more correlations above $+0.5$, and the large sample studies report more correlations between -0.2 and $+0.2$. Both differences fit the rationale that researchers make additional observations when they are observing correlations near zero. Some researchers predict the magnitudes of relationships and try to obtain enough observations to produce statistical significance (Cohen 1977); other researchers keep adding observations until they achieve statistical significance for some relationships; and still other researchers stop making observations when they obtain large positive correlations. Because large sample studies and small sample studies do differ little in the data they produce, an emphasis on statistical significance amounts to an emphasis on absolutely small correlations. As a result of our analysis, I view reports of 'not statistically significant' as statements about the amount and appropriateness of the analyzed data rather than statements about the meaningfulness of observed phenomena.

A variety of alternative measures for effect sizes have been proposed (Glass, McGraw, and Smith 1981; Hunter and Schmidt 1990; Snyder and Lawson 1993; Tatsuoka 1993; Fleiss 1994; Rosenthal 1994; Kileen, 2005). Effect sizes are useful both because they are continuous variables rather than binary ones and because their magnitudes relate directly to influence on dependent variables. Two-dozen education and psychology journals now insist that researchers report effect sizes. However, to represent an estimate (of any sort) by a single number overstates the precision of that number. Therefore, advocates of statistical reform typically urge researchers to report confidence intervals for effect sizes rather than point estimates of them (Thompson 2002; also see Rosenthal and Rubin 1994). The advantage of this approach is that it describes an effect size as having a wide range when there is ambiguity. The disadvantage of this approach is that it tends to convert a continuous variable (effect size) into a binary one when researchers revert to saying that the confidence intervals do or do not encompass zero.

One stimulus for increasing attention to effect sizes has been meta-analysis, the statistical analysis of comparable findings from numerous studies. Since any individual study is liable to produce idiosyncratic findings, comparisons of many studies can help to average out the peculiarities of individual studies, and may allow inferences about the reasons for variations across studies. Such comparisons have been occurring for decades under the headings of literature reviews or theoretical syntheses, and meta-analyses attempt to systematize and quantify them.

Meta-analysis fosters the reporting of effect sizes because statistical comparisons across studies need measures that are standardized, and effect sizes such as standardized regression coefficients appear to be standardized. However, those who have performed meta-analyses have not always considered the probable differences among studies that arise from factors that influence the observed variability. For example, data gathered at a single site that has low turnover of personnel might have variances that are reduced by shared experiences, shared culture, and shared policies and procedures: Merely standardizing such data does not make them comparable with data gathered across many diverse sites.

Some of the inferences made in meta-analyses are subject to the outlier effects that require large sample sizes for reliable inferences from regression analyses. Suppose that a meta-analysis examines fifty studies, each of which has 100 observations. The reliability of some inferences, such as the average values of coefficients across the fifty studies, approaches that of a very large sample ($50 * 100 = 5,000$). However, for inferences about the reasons why studies obtained different findings, the sample size is only fifty, which is far too few for ordinary least-squares statistics, so reliability is poor. The studies discussed in the previous chapter (Schmidt 1971; Claudy 1972; Einhorn and Hogarth, 1975; Dorans and Drasgow 1978) say researchers should have at least 100–200 studies in hand for inferences about the differences among past studies; and for inferences that might apply reliably to future studies, researchers should have at least 200–400 studies in hand. Even with these sample sizes, however, inferences from meta-analyses will only be approximately as reliable as the analysts' a priori hypotheses. Truly informative inferences about the differences among studies included in a meta-analysis would seem to require many hundreds or even thousands of studies. Since many existing meta-analyses have examined fewer than 100 studies, their authors might more usefully have published their hypotheses about the properties of studies without trying to support them with insufficient data.

5.3.3 Robust Statistics

Errors in data also threaten statistical inferences. Audits of widely available databases have found error rates approaching 30 percent, and experiences have convinced me that data gathered by students also contain numerous errors. Statisticians assess inference techniques in terms of their breakdown points—the smallest numbers of erroneous observations that can utterly invalidate computed statistics. Table 5.1 shows the breakdown points for five regression methods. Squared-error statistics have a breakdown point of only one observation, meaning that a single bad observation, which could be a data entry error, can greatly distort a computation.

Any statistical inference or test is only as meaningful as the compared subpopulations are homogeneous, but data are very often non-homogeneous. That is, observations classified as representing a single

Table 5.1 Breakdown points: Smallest numbers of observations that can distort analysis

Ordinary least squares regression (OLS)	1 observation
Absolute-error regression (L1)	1 observation
Least median squares regression (LMS)	Up to 50 percent of the observations
Least trimmed squares regression (LTS)	Up to 50 percent of the observations
Robust MM regression	Up to 50 percent of the observations

thing actually represent mixtures of different things. Indeed, because every person and social system is idiosyncratic in one aspect or another, there are many alternative ways to classify observations. For instance, the preceding section pointed out that Wachtell, Lipton, Rosen, and Katz differs greatly from other law firms. Theories that appear to describe most law firms fairly well do not describe Wachtell well; and if one includes Wachtell in the category 'law firms', Wachtell becomes an outlier that can strongly affect any statistical inferences about 'law firms'. If one includes Wachtell in the category 'exceptional law firms', Wachtell is still an outlier but a less extreme one. Theories that seem to describe most exceptional law firms fairly well do not describe Wachtell well, and Wachtell can strongly affect any statistical inferences about 'exceptional law firms'. Therefore, it is very important to make decisions about categorization that do not distort statistical inferences. Such decisions are fairly easy when only two or three variables are involved, but they become increasingly difficult as the numbers of variables increase because people lack the ability to visualize four or more dimensions. For that reason, statisticians have developed statistical methods that classify observations on the basis of computations. For example, one exhaustive procedure examines all possible subsets that comprise, say, 90 percent of the data and chooses the subset that is most compact.

Four of the methods listed in Table 5.1 are said to be 'robust' because they are less sensitive to data errors and extreme anomalies than ordinary squared-error regression. Absolute-error regression (L1) is less sensitive to extreme anomalies because it sums the absolute values of deviations from regression lines rather than the squared values (see Figure 4.6). However, like OLS regression, absolute-error regression has a breakdown point of only one observation, whereas the other three methods offer the possibility of drawing reliable inferences from noisy data. Least median squares (LMS) regression is extremely insensitive to erroneous data or extreme anomalies because it ignores all of the observations that lie some distance from regression lines. The corresponding disadvantage of LMS regression is that it pays no attention to most observations. Least trimmed squares (LTS) regression resembles OLS regression except that it ignores a user-defined fraction of the outlying observations. Because the ignored fraction is arbitrary, it makes sense to compare the results of computations omitting different fractions. Robust MM regression resembles OLS regression except that it limits the influence of outlying observations instead of ignoring them.

To illustrate these various methods, I constructed 12,000 synthetic observations of a dependent variable and five independent variables. All six variables contain measurement errors, a few observations have data entry errors that shift the decimal point one digit left or right, and three of the independent variables have skewed distributions. Table 5.2 shows performance statistics for the methods in Table 5.1. With moderately noisy data, all of the robust methods yield more accurate estimates than does OLS, the most accurate methods being LTS and Robust MM regression. However, no statistical method can extract plausible estimates from very noisy data. Large measurement errors and numerous data entry errors break up the associations between the dependent and independent variables and make all of the independent variables look more similar to each other. Thus, regression estimates overstate the ordinate and understate the coefficients of the independent variables, especially the more influential ones. Table 5.2 shows that coefficient estimates from very noisy data are useless no matter what analytic method is used.

Robustness can mean that these methods yield inferences that are more reliable. Because squared-error statistics (e.g. OLS regression) demand sample sizes much larger than many studies can achieve, researchers need inference methods that can draw reliable inferences from samples of the sizes that are practically achievable. Robust methods that have high breakdown points may be able to draw reliable inferences even if many observations are erroneous. However, the relationships between sample size and inferential accuracy are not

Table 5.2 Average absolute percentage error in estimated coefficients

Estimation method	Moderately noisy data	Very noisy data
Ordinary least squares regression (OLS)	67.8%	85.9%
Absolute-error regression (L1)	25.3%	83.3%
Least median squares regression (LMS)	12.9%	83.0%
Least trimmed squares regression (LTS) with 90% of the data	9.9%	91.1%
Least trimmed squares regression (LTS) with 80% of the data	8.3%	78.5%
Robust MM regression	8.2%	82.5%
Robust MM regression with 90% of the data	8.3%	83.1%

simple because smaller samples have lower probabilities of including rare errors. Suppose, for example, that the probability of a data entry error is 1 percent. The probability that a sample of 100 would include no such errors is 7 percent, whereas the probability that a sample of 1,000 would include no such errors is nearly zero.

Figure 5.1 shows the comparative accuracy of coefficient estimates made with OLS versus Robust MM regression. The variables in these synthesized data have Normal distributions and contain measurement errors, and a few observations have data entry errors that shift the decimal point one digit left or right. Each point represents twenty samples, and the lines represent the median percentage errors and the upper and lower quartiles around this median. The advantage of using robust statistical methods is obvious, and this advantage increases with smaller samples.

Many researchers appear to believe that a regression that 'explains' a higher percentage of the variance has greater credibility. At least with OLS regression, this is a debatable assumption. Figure 5.2 relates the median percentage errors in estimated coefficients to the percentage of variance explained for the regressions that generated Figure 5.1. Figure 5.1 shows, some calculations with samples of size 50 and 100 yielded very erroneous coefficient estimates, with the result that

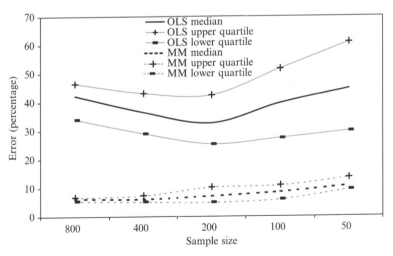

Figure 5.1 Errors in estimated coefficients

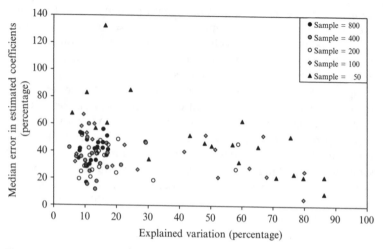

Figure 5.2 Median errors in estimated coefficients versus explained variation with OLS

median percentage errors do correlate negatively with explained variation for samples of size 50 and 100. However, for samples of size 200 or more, there is no correlation between explained variation and median percentage errors.

The superior accuracy of robust statistical methods is evident, and since both Robust MM regression and LTS regression produce the same results as OLS when data match the assumptions of OLS, there is never a reason to prefer OLS as a way to estimate parameters. Likewise, likelihood ratios and effect sizes are much more meaningful than statistical significance tests. Data that do not have perfect Normal distributions do imply a need to use simulation to compare alternative models, say by estimating likelihood ratios. Although such simulations are not as convenient as looking up numbers in tables, they should add only a few days work to a research study, a small price to pay for more convincing results.

5.4 Building Consensus

Social processes offer both opportunities and discouraging prospects for the production of knowledge. Opportunities come from the possibility of exerting influence—influence over social norms for how research should be conducted, influence over the ideas that people accept as knowledge, and influence over one's own career. Those who dislike the existing norms can try to change them. Those who believe they have discovered valuable insights can try to persuade others of their value. Those who want to achieve renown or respect can take advantage of the prevailing norms.

Social processes influence both the conduct of research and the marketing of research findings to other people. Several studies have reported how scientists develop and interpret observations interactively with other people (Mitroff 1974; Latour and Woolgar 1979; Zukav 1979; Knorr-Cetina 1981). Other studies have described competition among researchers, secrecy, and misrepresented results (Gaston 1971; Gilbert 1977; Samuelson 1980; Over 1982).

Peter and Olson (1983: 111) urged social scientists to see research as 'the marketing of ideas in the form of substantive and methodological theories'. Authors need to win audiences for their work—to persuade potential readers to read their books and articles and to convince actual readers that the ideas and theories in their books and articles are plausible and useful. Social scientists who believe they have something valuable to contribute have to be willing to persuade others of this value; and to do that, they have to adapt their manuscripts to the perceptual frameworks of potential readers. Davis (1971) tried to identify properties that make contributions to sociology 'interesting', hence attracting attention and exerting influence. He inferred that 'interesting' books and articles exhibit presentational patterns that challenge readers to resolve apparent contradictions. One such pattern would be to assert that a phenomenon that seems to be peculiar to a specific local situation occurs quite generally; another such pattern would be to assert that a phenomenon that seems to be unstable and changing is actually stable and unchanging.

The social processes involved in the production of knowledge also create discouraging prospects insofar as produced knowledge is ephemeral, based mainly or wholly on contagion rather than truly useful insights. Because researchers need to believe they are pursuing potentially fruitful courses of action, they tend to join bandwagons. Jönsson and Lundin (1977) described the waves of enthusiasm that occur in small companies: Someone proposes a new product or strategic idea that others find attractive, so more and more people become proponents for this idea. Eventually, however, people begin to notice the disadvantages associated with this idea; fewer and fewer join the bandwagon and some proponents cease to support it. The number of proponents begins to decline... until someone proposes yet another new idea to replace the earlier one. It is easy to see such waves of enthusiasm in the social sciences. In organization studies, there have been contingency theory, population ecology, and institutional theory. In organizational behavior, there have been attribution theory, organizational citizenship behavior, and identity theory. In microeconomics, there have been the behavioral theory of the firm, game theory (twice), and agency theory. In sociology, there have been symbolic interactionism, ethnomethodology, and network theories. In statistical methods, there have been factor analysis, stepwise regression, autoregressive moving averages, logit and probit analyses, Heckman's method, and fixed-effects models.

Such waves of enthusiasm challenge researchers to maintain idealism and sincerity. It is far too easy for researchers to see the social sciences as mere games to be played for personal advantage such as the gaining of tenure or promotions or publishing in prestigious journals or even a sense of social belonging. Doctoral students want formulas that will yield career success, proven examples and recipes to follow. Researchers believe, or at least conjecture with trepidation, that their success depends on pursuing the currently fashionable topics and using the currently fashionable methods. Widely accepted methodological slogans create facades of wisdom.

For knowledge to develop, knowledge must actually exist, which means that there must be consensus that some things are known—paradigms (Pfeffer 1993). However, many contemporary research norms and practices impede the creation of consensus. Researchers promote their careers by proposing and marketing new ideas with which they are personally identified. Researchers who have proposed and marketed ideas defend them aggressively even if their ideas differ insignificantly from those of others. Before the social sciences can make real progress, social scientists will have to decide that successful careers and the maintenance of status hierarchies should take second place to revealing research designs and careful assessments of research contributions. Social scientists will have to decide that they actually want progress to occur in the overall body of knowledge. If Platt's (1964) conjectures are right, social scientists will have to recognize the value of demonstrating that some ideas are silly or meaningless and that many hypotheses are not useful additions to what is known. That is, social scientists will have to realize that effective paradigms identify some methodologies as ineffective, some issues as unimportant, and some questions as having already been answered satisfactorily.

As the preceding chapter described, Webster and I (1988) proposed that social scientists adopt and use sets of baseline propositions that delineate the agreed body of knowledge. For example, one such proposition might be 'Participation in the implementation of new ideas makes the ideas more acceptable'. An agreed body of knowledge is a prerequisite for incremental development because people cannot decide that a new proposition constitutes an increment until they know what the proposition is supposed to augment. However, Webster and I speculated that social scientists are extremely unlikely to agree about baseline propositions voluntarily. Many social scientists hold vested interests in specific propositions that do not qualify for baseline status or that would become redundant. Because social scientists are unaccustomed to projecting their ideas onto shared frameworks, they would have to learn new ways of thinking and speaking. Some social scientists have expressed doubts about the validity of theoretical propositions of any kind. Thus, we surmised that constructing consensus would require explicit actions by key journals that act as professional gatekeepers. Specifically, the key journals might adhere to three policies:

1. Journals should refuse to publish studies that purport to contradict the baseline propositions. Since the propositions are known laws of nature, valid evidence cannot contradict them. Apparent discrepancies from these laws point to exogenous influences, to interactions among influences, or to observational errors.

2. Journals should refuse to publish studies that do no more than reaffirm the baseline propositions. Known laws of nature need no more documentation. However, there may be need to explain the implications of these laws in circumstances where those implications are not self-evident.

3. Journals should insist that all published studies refer to any of the baseline propositions that are relevant. There is no need for new theoretical propositions where the existing laws are already adequate, so phenomena that can be explained by these laws must be so explained.

Would baseline propositions prove to be adequate laws in the long run? No, unquestionably they would not. Firstly, because we humans are simple creatures trying to comprehend complex worlds, it behooves us to expect our theories to be somewhat wrong; and because we are hopeful creatures, we aspire to do better. Secondly, in order to integrate multiple propositions, social sciences would have to move from less specific propositions to more specific ones. Attempts to apply baseline propositions would likely produce demands for standardized measures, and then more specific propositions. Thirdly, processes that tend to alter some characteristics of a social system also tend to evoke antithetical processes that affect these characteristics oppositely. Stability creates pressures for change, consensus arouses dissent, constraint stirs up rebellion, conformity brings out independence, and conviction evokes skepticism. Thus, the very existence of a scientific paradigm would call forth efforts to overthrow that paradigm.

There are inevitable trade-offs between innovation and the status quo. Any agreed body of knowledge must suppress some proposed innovations by defining them as not really innovative at all, and errors are inevitable when existing paradigms misunderstand genuine innovations. That is why scientific progress tends to oscillate between periods of incremental change and periods of dramatic reorientation. Nevertheless, an agreed body of knowledge makes progress possible by suppressing the proposed innovations that are actually noise and that make it difficult to distinguish genuine innovations.

5.5 How Well Can It Work?

Very substantial improvements are possible in the effectiveness of social science research. Some studies stand out as adventures into what is possible. Not only are there many ways to make improvements but also some prevalent techniques are remarkably ineffective, and many researchers use these ineffective tactics without being aware of their inadequacies. If researchers would use the most effective techniques available, fewer studies would report spurious findings and more studies would have lasting value.

Substantial improvements are, nevertheless, unlikely because they would require widespread and dramatic changes in practices and norms and they would upset people who have stakes in the present.

Fewer spurious findings would mean that researchers would have to do more work to complete each study. Articles would be longer and they might be fewer. Many researchers aspire to succeed in the social system that exists; few researchers have the confidence and conviction to discount the expectations of their colleagues or the demands of their employers.

Just as knowledge is a human production, serious impediments to developing knowledge are also produced by people. Prevalent research tactics are not intrinsically bad; rather, people apply them inappropriately and exploit their weaknesses. If researchers are to find better ways, they must do so willingly.

Despite my pessimism about prospects for wide-scale change, I nevertheless urge researchers to experiment with more productive research tactics at the margin. The challenges of producing knowledge about people and social systems are immense and changing, and they can only be surmounted by people who see social science research as a high calling that deserves their best efforts.

'Science becomes dangerous only when it imagines that it has reached its goal.'

—George Bernard Shaw (1911)

References

Abelson, R. P. (1997). 'On the Surprising Longevity of Flogged Horses: Why There is a Case for the Significance Test', *Psychological Science*, 8(1): 12–15.

—— Aronson, E., McGuire, W. J., Newcomb, T. M., Rosenberg, M. J., and Tannenbaum, P. H. (1968). *Theories of Cognitive Consistency*. Chicago: Rand-McNally.

Aldrich, H. E. (1972). 'Technology and Organizational Structure: A Reexamination of the Findings of the Aston Group', *Administrative Science Quarterly*, 17: 26–43.

Altheide, D. L. and Johnson, J. M. (1980). *Bureaucratic Propaganda*. Boston, MA: Allyn & Bacon.

Ames, E. and Reiter, S. (1961). 'Distributions of Correlation Coefficients in Economic Time Series', *Journal of the American Statistical Association*, 56: 637–56.

Andrews, P. W. S. (1949). 'A Reconsideration of the Theory of the Individual Business', *Oxford Economics Papers*, 1: 54–89.

Armstrong, J. S. (1985). *Long-Range Forecasting: From Crystal Ball to Computer*, 2nd edn. New York: Wiley-Interscience.

Ashby, R. W. (1961). *Introduction to Cybernetics*. London: Chapman & Hall.

Bales, R. F. (1953). 'The Equilibrium Problem in Small Groups', in T. Parsons, R. F. Bales, and E. A. Shils (eds.), *Working Papers in the Theory of Action*. Glencoe, IL: Free Press, pp. 111–61.

Barnard, C. I. (1937). *The Functions of the Executive*. Lectures presented at the Lowell Institute, Boston. An expanded version was published as a book in 1938; Cambridge, MA: Harvard University Press.

Barnett, M. L., Starbuck, W. H., and Pant, P. N. (2003). 'Which Dreams Come True? Endogeneity, Industry Structure, and Forecasting Accuracy', *Industrial and Corporate Change*, 12(4): 653–72.

Barnett, W. P. and Hansen, M. T. (1996). 'The Red Queen in Organizational Evolution', *Strategic Management Journal*, 17: 139–57.

Bazerman, M. H. (1997). *Judgment in Managerial Decision Making*, 2nd edn. New York: Wiley.

Berkson, J. (1938). 'Some Difficulties of Interpretation Encountered in the Application of the Chi-Square Test', *Journal of the American Statistical Association*, 33: 526–36.

References

Bettman, J. R. and Weitz, B. A. (1983). 'Attribution in the Board Room: Causal Reasoning in Corporate Annual Reports', *Administrative Science Quarterly*, 28: 165–83.

Beyer, J. M. (1981). 'Ideologies, Values, and Decision Making in Organizations', in P. C. Nystrom and W. H. Starbuck (eds.), *Handbook of Organizational Design, Vol. 2*. New York: Oxford University Press, pp. 167–202.

Blaug, M. (1980). *The Methodology of Economics: Or How Economists Explain*. Cambridge: Cambridge University Press.

Boland, R. J., Jr. (1982). 'Myth and Technology in the American Accounting Profession', *Journal of Management Studies*, 19: 109–27.

Bonini, C. P. (1963). *Simulation of Information and Decision Systems in the Firm*. Englewood Cliffs, NJ: Prentice-Hall.

Box, G. E. P. and Draper, N. R. (1969). *Evolutionary Operation*. New York: Wiley.

Boyce, J. E. (1955). 'Comparison of Methods of Combining Scores to Predict Academic Success in a Cooperative Engineering Program'. Ph.D. thesis, Purdue University.

Brodie, R. J. and de Kluyver, C. A. (1987). 'A Comparison of the Short Term Forecasting Accuracy of Econometric and Naive Extrapolation Models of Market Share', *International Journal of Forecasting*, 3: 423–37.

Brunsson, N. (1982). 'The Irrationality of Action and Action Rationality: Decisions, Ideologies, and Organisational Actions', *Journal of Management Studies*, 19: 29–44.

Calhoun, M. A. and Starbuck, W. H. (2003). 'Barriers to Creating Knowledge', in M. Easterby-Smith and M. A. Lyles (eds.), *Handbook of Organizational Learning and Knowledge Management*. Oxford: Blackwell, pp. 473–92.

Campbell, D. T. and Russo, M. J. (1998). *Social Experimentation*. London: Sage.

Campbell, J. H. (1985). 'An Organizational Interpretation of Evolution', in D. J. Depew and B. H. Weber (eds.), *Evolution at a Crossroads: The New Biology and the New Philosophy of Science*. Cambridge, MA: MIT Press, pp. 133–68.

Campbell, J. P. (1982). 'Editorial: Some Remarks from the Outgoing Editor', *Journal of Applied Psychology*, 67: 691–700.

—— Daft, R. L., and Hulin, C. L. (1982). *What to Study: Generating and Developing Research Questions*. Beverly Hills, CA: Sage.

Cappelli, P. and Sherer P. D. (1991). 'The Missing Role of Context in OB: The Need for a Meso-level Approach', *Research in Organizational Behavior*, 13: 55–110.

Cartwright, D. and Harary, F. (1956). 'Structural Balance: A Generalization of Heider's Theory', *Psychological Review*, 63: 277–93.

—— and Zander, A. (1953). 'Leadership: Introduction', in D. Cartwright and A. Zander (eds.), *Group Dynamics*. Evanston, IL: Row, Peterson, pp. 535–50.

Cattell, R. B. and Stice, G. F. (1954). 'Four Formulae for Selecting Leaders on the Basis of Personality', *Human Relations*, 7: 493–507.

Chan, W. T. (1963). *Source Book in Chinese Philosophy*. Princeton, NJ: Princeton University Press.

Chomsky, N. (1959). 'A Review of B. F. Skinner's Verbal Behavior', *Language*, 35(1): 26–58.

Cicchetti, D. V. (1980). 'Reliability of Reviews for the *American Psychologist*', *American Psychologist*, 35: 300–3.

—— (1991). 'The Reliability of Peer Review for Manuscript and Grant Submissions: A Cross-Disciplinary Investigation', *Behavioral and Brain Sciences*, 14: 119–86 (includes 33 pages of comments by others and a response by Cicchetti).

—— and Eron, L. D. (1979). 'The Reliability of Manuscript Reviewing for the *Journal of Abnormal Psychology*', *Proceedings of the American Statistical Association (Social Statistics Section)*, 22: 596–600.

Claudy, J. G. (1972). 'A Comparison of Five Variable Weighting Procedures', *Educational and Psychological Measurement*, 32: 311–22.

Clemen, R. T. (1989). 'Combining Forecasts: A Review and Annotated Bibliography', *International Journal of Forecasting*, 5: 559–83.

Coch, L. and French, J. R. P., Jr. (1948). 'Overcoming Resistance to Change', *Human Relations*, 1: 512–32.

Cohen, J. (1977). *Statistical Power Analysis for the Behavioral Sciences*. New York: Academic Press.

—— (1994). 'The Earth is Round (p < .05)', *American Psychologist*, 49: 997–1003.

Cohen, M. D., March, J. G., and Olsen, J. P. (1972). 'A Garbage Can Model of Organizational Choice', *Administrative Science Quarterly*, 17: 1–25.

Coleman, J. S., Katz, E., and Menzel, H. (1966). *Medical Innovation*. Indianapolis: Bobbs-Merrill.

Connor, E. F. and Simberloff, D. (1983). 'Interspecific Competition and Species Co-occurrence Patterns on Islands: Null Models and the Evaluation of Evidence', *Oikos*, 41: 455–65.

—— —— (1986). 'Competition, Scientific Method, and Null Models in Ecology', *American Scientist*, 74: 155–62.

Cool, K. and Schendel, D. E. (1988). 'Performance Differences Among Strategic Group Members', *Strategic Management Journal*, 9: 207–23.

Cummings, L. L. and Schmidt, S. M. (1972). 'Managerial Attitudes of Greeks: The Roles of Culture and Industrialization', *Administrative Science Quarterly*, 17: 265–72.

Czarniawska, B. (2001). 'Is It Possible to be a Constructionist Consultant?', *Management Learning*, 32: 253–66.

Davis, M. S. (1971). 'That's Interesting! Towards a Phenomenology of Sociology and a Sociology of Phenomenology', *Philosophy of Social Science*, 1: 309–44.

Dawes, R. M. and Corrigan, B. (1974). 'Linear Models in Decision Making', *Psychological Bulletin*, 81: 95–106.

References

Deese, J. (1972). *Psychology as Science and Art*. New York: Harcourt.

Denrell, J. (2004). 'Random Walks and Sustained Competitive Advantage', *Management Science*, 50: 922–34.

Denzin, N. K. (1978). *The Research Act*, 2nd edn. New York: McGraw-Hill.

Diebold, J. (1952). *Automation, the Advent of the Automatic Factory*. New York: Van Nostrand.

Dorans, N. and Drasgow, F. (1978). 'Alternative Weighting Schemes for Linear Prediction', *Organizational Behavior and Human Performance*, 21: 316–45.

Downey, H. K., Hellriegel, D., and Slocum, J. W., Jr. (1975). 'Environmental Uncertainty: The Construct and Its Application', *Administrative Science Quarterly*, 20: 613–29.

—— Hellriegel, D., and Slocum, J. W., Jr. (1977). 'Individual Characteristics as Sources of Perceived Uncertainty', *Human Relations*, 30: 161–74.

Dreeben, R. (1968). *On What Is Learned in School*. Reading, MA: Addison-Wesley.

Dunbar, R. L. M. (1981). 'Designs for Organizational Control', in P. C. Nystrom and W. H. Starbuck (eds.), *Handbook of Organizational Design*, Vol. 2. New York: Oxford University Press, pp. 85–115.

—— and Goldberg, W. H. (1978). 'Crisis Development and Strategic Response in European Corporations', *Journal of Business Administration*, 9(2): 139–49.

Dutton, J. M. and Starbuck, W. H. (1967). 'How Charlie Estimates Run-Time', in M.P. Hottenstein and R.W. Millman (eds.), *Research Toward the Development of Management Thought*. Bowling Green, OH: Academy of Management, pp. 48–63.

—— and Starbuck, W. H. (1971a). *Computer Simulation of Human Behavior*. New York: Wiley.

—— and Starbuck, W. H. (1971b). 'Finding Charlie's Run-Time Estimator', in J. M. Dutton and W. H. Starbuck (eds.), *Computer Simulation of Human Behavior*. New York: Wiley, pp. 218–42.

Edelman, M. (1977). *Political Language: Words That Succeed and Policies That Fail*. New York: Academic Press.

Eden, D. and Ravid, G. (1982). 'Pygmalion Versus Self-Expectancy: Effects of Instructor-and Self-Expectancy on Trainee Performance', *Organizational Behavior and Human Performance*, 30: 351–64.

Edwards, W., Lindman, H., and Savage, L. J. (1963). 'Bayesian Statistical Inference for Psychological Research', *Psychological Review*, 70: 193–242.

Einhorn, H. J. and Hogarth, R. M. (1975). 'Unit Weighting Schemes for Decision Making', *Organizational Behavior and Human Performance*, 13: 171–92.

Elliott, J. W. (1973). 'A Direct Comparison of Short-Run GNP Forecasting Models', *Journal of Business*, 46: 33–60.

Ellison, G. (2002). 'The Slowdown of the Economics Publishing Process', *Journal of Political Economy*, 110: 947–93.

Estes, W. K. (1957). 'Theory of Learning with Constant, Variable, or Contingent Probabilities of Reinforcement', *Psychometrika*, 22: 113–32.

—— (1997). 'Significance Testing in Psychological Research: Some Persisting Issues', *Psychological Science*, 8(1): 18–20.

Falk, R. and Greenbaum, C. W. (1995). 'Significance Tests Die Hard: The Amazing Persistence of a Probabilistic Misconception', *Theory & Psychology*, 5: 75–98.

Faust, D. (1984). *The Limits of Scientific Reasoning*. Minneapolis, MN: University of Minnesota Press.

Faust, R. E. (1978). 'Emerging Challenges for the Research Scientist', *Research Management*, 21(3): 39–42.

Festinger, L. (1957). *A Theory of Cognitive Dissonance*. Evanston, IL: Row, Peterson.

Fidler, F., Thomason, N., Cumming, G., Finch, S., and Leeman, J. (2004). 'Editors can Lead Researchers to Confidence Intervals, But can't Make Them Think', *Psychological Science*, 15: 119–26.

Fiedler, F. E. (1967). *A Theory of Leadership Effectiveness*. New York: McGraw-Hill.

Fischhoff, B. (1980). 'For Those Condemned to Study the Past: Heuristics and Biases in Hindsight', in D. Kahneman, P. Slovic, and A. Tversky (eds.), *Judgment Under Uncertainty: Heuristics and Biases*. Cambridge: Cambridge University Press, pp. 335–51.

Fleishman, E. A., Harris, E. F., and Burtt, H. E. (1955). *Leadership and Supervision in Industry*. Columbus, OH: Ohio State University, Bureau of Educational Research.

Fleiss, J. L. (1994). 'Measures of Effect Size for Categorical Data', in H. Cooper and L. V. Hedges (eds.), *The Handbook of Research Synthesis*. New York: Sage, pp. 245–60.

Fromkin, H. L. (1969). 'The Behavioral Science Laboratories at Purdue's Krannert School', *Administrative Science Quarterly*, 14: 171–77.

Garvey, W. D., Lin, N., and Nelson, C. E. (1970). 'Some Comparisons of Communication Activities in the Physical and Social Sciences', in C. E. Nelson and D. K. Pollock (eds.), *Communications among Scientists and Engineers*. Lexington, MA: Heath Lexington, pp. 61–84.

Gaston, J. (1971). 'Secretiveness and Competition for Priority of Discovery in Physics', *Minerva*, 9: 472–92.

George, C. S., Jr. (1968). *The History of Management Thought*. Englewood Cliffs, NJ: Prentice-Hall.

Gibb, C. A. (1954). 'Leadership', in G. Lindzey (ed.), *Handbook of Social Psychology*. Cambridge, MA: Addison-Wesley.

Gilbert, N. G. (1977). 'Referencing as Persuasion', *Social Studies of Science*, 7: 113–22.

Gilpin, M. E. and Diamond, J. M. (1984). 'Are Serious Co-occurrences on Islands Non-random, and are Null Hypotheses Useful in Community

Ecology?', in D. R. Strong L. Abele, and A. R. Thistle (eds.), *Ecological Communities: Conceptual Issues and the Evidence*. Princeton, NJ: Princeton University Press, pp. 297–315.

Gilson, R. J. and Mnookin, R. H. (1989). 'Coming of Age in a Corporate Law Firm: The Economics of Associate Career Patterns', *Stanford Law Review*, 41: 567–95.

Glass, G. V., McGraw, B., and Smith, M. L. (1981). *Meta-analysis in Social Research*. Beverly Hills, CA: Sage.

Goldberg, L. R. (1970). 'Man Versus Model of Man: A Rationale, Plus Some Evidence, for a Method of Improving on Clinical Inferences', *Psychological Bulletin*, 73: 422–32.

Gordon, G. and Marquis, S. (1966). 'Freedom, Visibility, of Consequences, and Scientific Innovation', *American Journal of Sociology*, 72: 195–202.

Gottfredson, D. M. and Gottfredson, S. D. (1982). 'Criminal Justice and (Reviewer) Behavior: How to Get Papers Published', *Criminal Justice and Behavior*, 9(3): 259–72.

Gottfredson, S. D. (1977). 'Scientific Quality and Peer-Group Consensus', Ph.D. thesis, Johns Hopkins University. (Dissertation Abstracts International, 38: 1950B.)

—— (1978). 'Evaluating Psychological Research Reports: Dimensions, Reliability, and Correlates of Quality Judgments', *American Psychologist*, 33(10): 920–34.

Greenwald, A. G. (1975). 'Consequences of Prejudice Against the Null Hypothesis', *Psychological Bulletin*, 82: 1–20.

Grinyer, P. H. and Norburn, D. (1975). 'Formal Strategizing for Existing Markets: Perceptions of Executives and Financial Performance', *Journal of the Royal Statistical Society, Series A*, 138: 70–97.

Guthrie, E. R. and Horton, G. P. (1946). *Cats in a Puzzle Box*. New York: Rinehart and Co.

Haire, M., Ghiselli, E. E., and Porter, L. W. (1966). *Managerial Thinking*. New York: Wiley.

Hargens, L. L. and Herting, J. R. (1990). 'Neglected Considerations in the Analysis of Agreement Among Journal Referees', *Scientometrics*, 19: 91–106.

Harris, R. J. (1997). 'Significance Tests have Their Place', *Psychological Science*, 8(1): 8–11.

Harvey, P. H., Colwell, R. K., Silvertown, J. W., and May, R. M. (1983). 'Null Models in Ecology', *Annual Review of Ecology and Systematics*, 14: 189–211.

Hatten, K. J. and Schendel, D. E. (1977). 'Heterogeneity Within an Industry: Firm Conduct in the U.S. Brewing Industry, 1952–1971', *Journal of Industrial Economics*, 26: 97–113.

Hayek, F. A. von (1975). *The Pretence of Knowledge*. Stockholm: The Nobel Foundation.

Hedges, L. V. (1987). 'How Hard is Hard Science, How Soft is Soft Science?', *American Psychologist*, 42: 443–55.

Heider, F. (1958). *The Psychology of Interpersonal Relations*. New York: Wiley.

Hendrick, C. (1976). 'Editorial Comment', *Personality and Social Psychology Bulletin*, 2: 207–8.

—— (1977). 'Editorial Comment', *Personality and Social Psychology Bulletin*, 3: 1–2.

Hilton, G. (1972). 'Causal Inference Analysis: A Seductive Process', *Administrative Science Quarterly*, 17: 44–55.

Hirschman, A. O. (1970). *Exit, Voice and Loyalty*. Cambridge, MA: Harvard University Press.

Hofstede, G. H. (1967). *The Game of Budget Control*. Assen: Van Gorcum.

Homans, G. C. (1950). *The Human Group*. New York: Harcourt Brace.

Hopwood, A. G. (1972). 'An Empirical Study of the Role of Accounting Data in Performance Evaluation', *Empirical Research in Accounting: Selected Studies* (supplement to the *Journal of Accounting Research*), 10: 156–82.

Horrobin, D. F. (1990). 'The Philosophical Basis of Peer Review and the Suppression of Innovation', *Journal of the American Medical Association*, 263(10): 1438–41.

Hubbard, R. and Armstrong, J. S. (1992). 'Are Null Results Becoming an Endangered Species in Marketing?', *Marketing Letters*, 3(2): 127–36.

—— and Ryan, P. A. (2000). 'The Historical Growth of Statistical Significance Testing in Psychology—and Its Future Prospects', *Educational and Psychological Measurement*, 60: 661–81.

Hull, C. L. (1943). *Principles of Behavior*. New York: D. Appleton Century.

Hunter, J. E. (1997). 'Needed: A Ban on the Significance Test', *Psychological Science*, 8(1): 3–7.

—— and Schmidt, F. L. (1990). *Methods of Meta-analysis: Correcting Error and Bias in Research Findings*. Newbury Park, CA: Sage.

Industrial Democracy in Europe International Research Group (1981). *Industrial Democracy in Europe*. Oxford: Oxford University Press.

Jeffreys, W. H. and Berger, J. O. (1992). 'Ockham's Razor and Bayesian analysis', *American Scientist*, 80: 64–72.

Jick, T. D. (1979). 'Mixing Qualitative and Quantitative Methods: Triangulation in Action', *Administrative Science Quarterly*, 24: 602–11.

Jönsson, S. A. and Lundin, R. A. (1977). 'Myths and Wishful Thinking as Management Tools', in P. C. Nystrom and W. H. Starbuck (eds.), *Prescriptive Models of Organizations*. Amsterdam: North-Holland, pp. 157–70.

Karlgren, B. (1950). *The Book of Documents*. Stockholm Museum of Far Eastern Antiquities.

—— (1970). *Glosses on the Book of Documents*. Stockholm: Museum of Far Eastern Antiquities.

References

Kelley, H. H. and Thibaut, J. W. (1954). 'Experimental Studies of Group Problem Solving and Process', in G. Lindzey (ed.), *Handbook of Social Psychology*, Vol. 2. Cambridge, MA: Addison-Wesley, pp. 735–86.

Kelley, K. and Maxwell, S. E. (2003). 'Sample Size for Multiple Regression: Obtaining Regression Coefficients That are Accurate, Not Simply Significant', *Psychological Methods*, 8(3): 305–21.

Kiesler, C. A. (1971). *The Psychology of Commitment*. New York: Academic Press.

Kileen, P. R. (2005). 'An Alternative to Null-Hypothesis Significance Tests', *Psychological Science*, 16: 345–53.

King, A. S. (1974). 'Expectation Effects in Organizational Change', *Administrative Science Quarterly*, 19: 221–30.

Kirk, R. E. (1996). 'Practical Significance: A Concept Whose Time has Come', *Educational and Psychological Measurement*, 56: 746–59.

Klayman, J. and Ha, Y.-W. (1987). 'Confirmation, Disconfirmation, and Information in Hypothesis Testing', *Psychological Review*, 94: 211–28.

Knorr-Cetina, K. D. (1981). *The Manufacture of Knowledge: Toward a Constructivist and Contextual Theory of Science*. Oxford: Pergamon.

Kuhn, T. S. (1962). *The Structure of Scientific Revolutions*. Chicago, IL: University of Chicago Press.

Kunda, G. (1992). *Engineering Culture: Control and Commitment in a High-Tech Corporation*. Philadelphia, PA: Temple University Press.

Landy, F. J. and Vasey, J. (1984). 'Theory and Logic in Human Resources Research', in K. M. Rowland and G. R. Ferris (eds.), *Research in Personnel and Human Resources Management*. Greenwich, CT: JAI Press, pp. 1–34.

Latham, G. P. and Yukl, G. A. (1975). 'A Review of Research on the Application of Goal Setting in Organizations', *Academy of Management Journal*, 18: 824–45.

—— , Erez, M., and Locke, E. A. (1988). 'Resolving Scientific Disputes by the Joint Design of Crucial Experiments by the Antagonists: Application to the Erez–Latham Dispute Regarding Participation in Goal Setting', *Journal of Applied Psychology Monograph*, 73(4): 753–72.

Latour, B. (1987). *Science in Action*. Cambridge, MA: Harvard University Press.

—— and Woolgar, S. (1979). *Laboratory Life*. Beverly Hills, CA: Sage.

Lawler, E. E. III and Hackman, J. R. (1969). 'Impact of Employee Participation in the Development of Pay Incentive Plans: A Field Experiment', *Journal of Applied Psychology*, 53: 467–71.

Lawrence, P. R. and Lorsch, J. W. (1967). *Organization and Environment*. Boston, MA: Graduate School of Business Administration, Harvard University.

Lawshe, C. H. and Schucker, R. E. (1959). 'The Relative Efficiency of Four Test Weighting Methods in Multiple Prediction', *Educational and Psychological Measurement*, 19: 103–14.

Legge, J. (1865). *The Chinese Classics*. New York: Oxford University Press.

Lewin, K. (1943). 'Forces Behind Food Habits and Methods of Change', *National Research Council Bulletin*, 108: 35–65.

—— (1953). 'Studies in Group Decision', in D. Cartwright and A. Zander (eds.), *Group Dynamics*. Evanston, IL: Row, Peterson, pp. 287–301.

Lewis, M. W. and Grimes, A. J. (1999). 'Metatriangulation: Building Theory from Multiple Paradigms', *Academy of Management Review*, 24: 672–90.

Liden, R. C. and Graen, G. (1980). 'Generalizability of the Vertical Dyad Linkage Model of Leadership', *Academy of Management Journal*, 23: 451–65.

Locke, E. A. (1968). 'Toward a Theory of Task Motivation and Incentives', *Organizational Behavior and Human Performance*, 3: 157–89.

Loftus, E. F. (1979). 'The Malleability of Human Memory', *American Scientist*, 67: 312–20.

Loftus, G. R. (1996). 'Psychology will be a Much Better Science When We Change the Way We Analyze Data', *Current Directions in Psychological Science*, 5: 161–71.

Lovell, M. C. (1983). 'Data Mining', *Review of Economics and Statistics*, 65: 1–12.

Luce, R. D. and Galanter, E. (1963). 'Discrimination', in R. D. Luce, R. A. Bush, and E. Galanter (eds.), *Handbook of Mathematical Psychology*, Vol. 1. New York: Wiley, pp. 191–243.

Mach, E. (1905). *Erkenntnis und Irrtum; Skizzen zur Psychologie der Forschung* [Knowledge and Error; Outlines for the Psychology of Research]. Originally published in 1905. Reprinted in 1987 by Wissenschaftliche Buchgesellschaft, Darmstadt.

Mahoney, M. J. (1977). 'Publication Prejudices: An Experimental Study of Confirmatory Bias in the Peer Review System', *Cognitive Therapy and Research*, 1: 161–75.

—— (1979). 'Psychology of the Scientist: An Evaluative Review', *Social Studies of Science*, 9(3): 349–75.

—— , Kazdin, A. E., and Kenigsberg, M. (1978). 'Getting Published', *Cognitive Therapy and Research*, 2: 69–70.

Maier, N. R. F. (1963). *Problem-Solving Discussions and Conferences: Leadership Methods and Skills*. New York: McGraw-Hill.

Makridakis, S. and Hibon, M. (1979). 'Accuracy of Forecasting: An Empirical Investigation', *Journal of the Royal Statistical Society, Series A*, 142: 97–145.

—— and Winkler, R. L. (1983). 'Averages of Forecasts: Some Empirical Results', *Management Science*, 29: 983–96.

—— , Andersen, A., Carbone, R., Fildes, R., Hibon, M., Lewandowski, R., Newton, J., Parzen, E., and Winkler, R. L. (1982). 'The Accuracy of Extrapolation (Time Series) Methods: Results of a Forecasting Competition', *Journal of Forecasting*, 1: 111–53.

Marrow, A. J., Bowers, D. G., and Seashore, S. E. (1967). *Management by Participation*. New York: Harper & Row.

Marsh, H. W. and Ball, S. (1981). 'Interjudgmental Reliability of Review for the *Journal of Educational Psychology*', *Journal of Educational Psychology*, 73: 872–80.

Martinez, B. (2004). 'Spitzer Charges Glaxo Concealed Paxil Data', *Wall Street Journal*, June 3: B1–2.

Marx, K. (1904). *A Contribution to the Critique of Political Economy*. Chicago, IL: Kerr. First published in 1859.

Mayo, E. (1946). *The Human Problems of an Industrial Civilization*. Boston, MA: Harvard University Press, Graduate School of Business Administration.

Meehl, P. E. (1954). *Clinical Versus Statistical Prediction: A Theoretical Analysis and Review of the Evidence*. Minneapolis, MN: University of Minnesota Press.

Meier, B. (2004*a*). 'Two Studies, Two Results, and a Debate Over a Drug', *New York Times*, June 3: C1 and C4.

—— (2004*b*). 'A Medical Journal Quandary: How to Report on Drug Trials', *New York Times*, June 21.

Meyer, A. D. (1982*a*). 'How Ideologies Supplant Formal Structures and Shape Responses to Environments', *Journal of Management Studies*, 19: 45–61.

—— (1982*b*). 'Adapting to Environmental Jolts', *Administrative Science Quarterly*, 27: 515–37.

Meyer, J. W. and Rowan, B. (1977). 'Institutionalized Organizations: Formal Structure as Myth and Ceremony', *American Journal of Sociology*, 83: 340–63.

Mezias, J. M. and Starbuck, W. H. (2003). 'Studying the Accuracy of Managers' Perceptions: A Research Odyssey', *British Journal of Management*, 14: 3–17.

Miller, D. (1990). *The Icarus Paradox: How Exceptional Companies Bring About Their Own Downfall*. New York: HarperCollins.

Mitroff, I. I. (1974). 'Norms and Counter-Norms in a Select Group of Apollo Moon Scientists: A Case Study of the Ambivalence of Scientists', *American Sociological Review*, 39: 579–95.

Newell, A. and Simon, H. A. (1956). 'The Logic Theory Machine, a Complex Information Processing System', *IEEE Transactions on Information Theory*, IT-2(3): S61–79.

——, Shaw, J. C., and Simon, H. A. (1958). 'Chess-Playing Programs and the Problem of Complexity', *IBM Journal of Research and Development*, 2(4): 320–35.

Nisbett, R. E. and Wilson, T. D. (1977). 'Telling More Than We can Know: Verbal Reports on Mental Processes', *Psychological Review*, 84: 231–59.

Nix, T. W. and Barnette, J. J. (1998). 'The Data Analysis Dilemma: Ban or Abandon. A Review of Null Hypothesis Significance Testing', *Research in the Schools*, 5(2): 3–15.

Normann, R. (1971). 'Organizational Innovativeness: Product Variation and Reorientation', *Administrative Science Quarterly*, 16: 203–15.

Nunnally, J. C. (1960). 'The Place of Statistics in Psychology', *Educational and Psychological Measurement*, 20: 641–50.

Nylenna, M., Riis, P., and Karlsson, Y. (1994). 'Multiple Blinded Reviews of the Same Two Manuscripts: Effects of Referee Characteristics and Publication Language', *Journal of the American Medical Association*, 272: 149–51.

Nystrom, P. C. and Starbuck, W. H. (eds.) (1981). *Handbook of Organizational Design*, 2 vols. New York: Oxford University Press.

—— and Starbuck, W. H. (1984). 'Organizational Facades', *Academy of Management, Proceedings of the Annual Meeting, Boston, 1984*: 182–85.

Orwin, R. G. and Cordray, D. S. (1985). 'Effects of Deficient Reporting on Meta-analysis: A Conceptual Framework and Reanalysis', *Psychological Bulletin*, 97: 134–47.

Over, R. (1982). 'Collaborative Research and Publication in Psychology', *American Psychologist*, 37: 996–1001.

Pant, P. N. and Starbuck, W. H. (1990). 'Innocents in the Forest: Forecasting and Research Methods', *Journal of Management*, 16: 433–60.

Payne, R. L. and Pugh, D. S. (1976). 'Organizational Structure and Climate', in M. D. Dunnette (ed.), *Handbook of Industrial and Organizational Psychology*. Chicago: Rand McNally, pp. 1125–73.

Peach, J. T. and Webb, J. L. (1983). 'Randomly Specified Macroeconomic Models: Some Implications for Model Selection', *Journal of Economic Issues*, 17: 697–720.

Penrose, E. T. (1959). *The Theory of the Growth of the Firm*. New York: Wiley.

Perloff, R. (1951). 'Using Trend-Fitting Predictor Weights to Improve Cross-Validation'. Ph.D. thesis, The Ohio State University.

Perrow, C. (1984). *Normal Accidents: Living with High-Risk Technologies*. New York: Basic Books.

Peter, J. P. and Olson, J. C. (1983). 'Is Science Marketing?', *Journal of Marketing*, 47: 111–25.

Peters, D. P. and Ceci, S. J. (1982). 'Peer-Review Practices of Psychological Journals: The Fate of Published Articles, Submitted Again', *Behavioral and Brain Sciences*, 5: 187–255 (includes 50 pages of comments by others and a response by Peters and Ceci).

Pfeffer, J. (1993). 'Barriers to the Advance of Organization Science: Paradigm Development as a Dependent Variable', *Academy of Management Review*, 18: 599–620.

Platt, J. R. (1964). 'Strong Inference', *Science*, 146: 347–53.

Polanyi, M. (1962). *Personal Knowledge*. London: Routledge.

Popper, K. R. (1959). *The Logic of Scientific Discovery*. New York: Basic Books.

Pratt, J. W., Raiffa, H., and Schlaifer, R. (1995). *Introduction to Statistical Decision Theory*. Cambridge, MA: MIT Press.

Pugh, D. S. (1981). 'The Aston Program of Research: Retrospect and Prospect', in A. Van de Ven and W. Joyce (eds.), *Perspectives on Organization Design and Behavior*. New York: Wiley, pp. 135–66.

References

Pugh, D. S., Hickson, D. J., Hinings, C. R., and Turner, C. (1968). 'Dimensions of Organization Structure', *Administrative Science Quarterly*, 13: 65–05.

Riecken, H. W. and Boruch, R. F. (eds.) (1974). *Social Experimentation: A Method for Planning and Evaluating Social Intervention*. Written by a committee of the Social Science Research Council. New York: Academic Press.

Rindova, V. P. and Starbuck, W. H. (1997a). 'Ancient Chinese Theories of Control', *Journal of Management Inquiry*, 6: 144–59.

—— and Starbuck, W. H. (1997b). 'Distrust in Dependence: The Ancient Challenge of Superior–Subordinate Relations', in T. A. R. Clark (ed.), *Advancements in Organization Behaviour: Essays in Honour of Derek Pugh*. Aldershot, Hants: Dartmouth Publishing.

Rivlin, A. M. and Timpane, P. M. (eds.) (1975). *Ethical and Legal Issues of Social Experimentation*. Washington, DC: Brookings Institution.

Robins, R. W., Gosling, S. D., and Craik, K. H. (1998). 'Psychological Science at the Crossroads', *American Scientist*, 86: 310–13.

Robinson, W. S. (1950). 'Ecological Correlations and the Behavior of Individuals', *American Sociological Review*, 15: 352–7.

Roethlisberger, F. J. and Dickson, W. J. (1939). *Management and the Worker*. Cambridge, MA: Harvard University Press.

Rosenberg, B. and Houghlet, M. (1974). 'Error Rates in CRSP and Compustat Databases and Their Implications', *Journal of Finance*, 29: 1303–10.

Rosenthal, R. (1994). 'Parametric Measures of Effect Size', in H. Cooper and L. V. Hedges (eds.), *The Handbook of Research Synthesis*. New York: Sage, pp. 231–44.

—— and Rubin, D. B. (1994). 'The Counternull Value of an Effect Size: A New Statistic', *Psychological Science*, 5: 329–34.

Rousseeuw, P. J. (1991). 'Why the Wrong Papers Get Published', *Chance: New Directions for Statistics and Computing*, 4(1): 41–3.

Sampson, E. E. (1969). 'Studies in Status Congruence', in L. Berkowitz (ed.), *Advances in Experimental Social Psychology*. New York: Academic Press, pp. 225–70.

Samuelson, F. (1980). 'J. B. Watson's Little Albert, Cyril Burt's Twins, and the Need for a Critical Science', *American Psychologist*, 35(6): 19–25.

Samuelson, S. S. and Jaffe, L. J. (1990). 'A Statistical Analysis of Law Firm Profitability', *Boston University Law Review*, 70: 185–211.

San Miguel, J. G. (1977). 'The Reliability of R&D Data in Compustat and 10-K Reports', *Accounting Review*, 52: 638–41.

Scarr, S. (1997). 'Rules of Evidence: A Larger Context for the Statistical Debate', *Psychological Science*, 8(1): 16–17.

—— and Weber, B. L. R. (1978). 'The reliability of Reviews for the *American Psychologist*', *American Psychologist*, 33: 935.

Schendel, D. and Patton, R. (1978). 'A Simultaneous Equation Model of Corporate Strategy', *Management Science*, 24: 1611–21.

Schlaifer, R. (1959). *Probability and Statistics for Business Decisions*. New York: McGraw-Hill.

Schmidt, F. L. (1971). 'The Relative Efficiency of Regression and Simple Unit Predictor Weights in Applied Differential Psychology', *Educational and Psychological Measurement*, 31: 699–714.

—— (1996). 'Statistical Significance Testing and Cumulative Knowledge in Psychology: Implications for the Training of Researchers', *Psychological Methods*, 1(2): 115–29.

Scott, W. A. (1974). 'Interreferee Agreement on Some Characteristics of Manuscripts Submitted to the *Journal of Personality and Social Psychology*', *American Psychologist*, 29: 698–702.

Seashore, S. E. (1954). *Group Cohesiveness in the Industrial Work Group*. Ann Arbor, MI: Institute for Social Research.

Shaw, G. B. (1911). 'On Doctors: Preface to "The Doctor's Dilemma" '. Reprinted in *Bernard Shaw: The Complete Prefaces, Volume 1: 1889–1913*. London: Allen Lane, 1993. (The quotation is on page 406 in the 1993 reprint.)

Shrout, P. E. (1997). 'Should Significance Tests be Banned?', *Psychological Science*, 8(1): 1–2.

Simon, H. A. (1944). 'Decision Making and Administrative Organization', *Public Administration Review*, 4: 16–30.

—— (1950). 'Modern Organization Theories', *Advanced Management*, 15(10): 2–4.

—— (1952). 'Comments on the Theory of Organizations', *American Political Science Review*, 46: 1130–9.

Singer, B. and Benassi, V. A. (1981). 'Occult Beliefs', *American Scientist*, 69(1): 49–55.

Skinner, B. F. (1953). *Science and Human Behavior*. New York: Macmillan.

Smedslund, J. (1984). 'What is Necessarily True in Psychology?', in J. R. Royce and L. P. Mos (eds.), *Annals of Theoretical Psychology*. New York: Plenum Press, pp. 241–72.

Smigel, E. D. and Ross, H. L. (1970). 'Factors in the Editorial Decision', *American Sociologist*, 5: 19–21.

Snyder, M. (1981). 'Seek, and ye shall Find: Testing Hypotheses About Other People', in E. T. Higgins, C. P. Herman, and M. P. Zanna (eds.), *Social Cognition, The Ontario Symposium*, Vol. 1. Hillsdale, NJ: Erlbaum, pp. 277–303.

Snyder, P. and Lawson, S. (1993). 'Evaluating Results Using Corrected and Uncorrected Effect Size Estimates', *Journal of Experimental Education*, 61: 334–49.

Solow, R. M. (1957). 'Technical Change and the Aggregate Production Function', *Review of Economics and Statistics*, 39(3), 312–20.

Stagner, R. (1982). 'Past and Future of Industrial/Organizational Psychology', *Professional Psychology*, 13: 892–902.

Starbuck, W. H. (1964). 'The Aspiration Mechanism', *General Systems*, 9: 191–203.

References

Starbuck, W. H. (1965). 'Organizational Growth and Development', in J. G. March (ed.), *Handbook of Organizations*. Chicago, IL: Rand McNally, 451–533.

—— (1968). 'Organizational Metamorphosis', in R. W. Millman and M. P. Hottenstein (eds.), *Promising Research Directions*. State College, PA: Academy of Management, pp. 113–22.

—— (1973). 'Tadpoles into Armageddon and Chrysler into Butterflies', *Social Science Research*, 2: 81–109.

—— (1974). 'The Current State of Organization Theory', in J. W. McGuire (ed.), *Contemporary Management: Issues and Viewpoints*. Englewood Cliffs, NJ: Prentice-Hall, pp. 123–39.

—— (1976). 'Organizations and Their Environments', in M. D. Dunnette (ed.), *Handbook of Industrial and Organizational Psychology*. Chicago, IL: Rand McNally, pp. 1069–123.

—— (1981). 'A Trip to View the Elephants and Rattlesnakes in the Garden of Aston', in A. H. Van de Ven and W. F. Joyce (eds.), *Perspectives on Organization Design and Behavior*. New York: Wiley, pp. 167–98.

—— (1983*a*). 'Computer Simulation of Human Behavior', *Behavioral Science*, 28: 154–65.

—— (1983*b*). 'Organizations as Action Generators', *American Sociological Review*, 48: 91–102.

—— (1985). 'Acting First and Thinking Later: Finding Decisions and Strategies in the Past', in J. M. Pennings (ed.), *Organizational Strategy and Change*. San Francisco: Jossey-Bass, pp. 336–72.

—— (1988). 'Surmounting Our Human Limitations', in R. Quinn and K. Cameron (eds.), *Paradox and Transformation: Toward a Theory of Change in Organization and Management*. Cambridge, MA: Ballinger.

—— (1989). 'Why Organizations Run into Crises ... and Sometimes Survive Them', in K. Laudon and J. Turner (eds.), *Information Technology and Management Strategy*. Englewood Cliffs, NJ: Prentice-Hall.

—— (1992*a*). 'Learning by Knowledge-Intensive Firms', *Journal of Management Studies*, 29(6): 713–40.

—— (1992*b*). 'Strategizing in the Real World', *International Journal of Technology Management, Special Publication on Technological Foundations of Strategic Management*, 8(1/2): 77–85.

—— (1993*a*). ' "Watch Where You Step!" or Indiana Starbuck Amid the Perils of Academe (Rated PG)', in A. Bedeian (ed.), *Management Laureates*, Vol. 3. Greenwich, CT: JAI Press, pp. 63–110.

—— (1993*b*). 'Keeping a Butterfly and an Elephant in a House of Cards: The Elements of Exceptional Success', *Journal of Management Studies*, 30: 885–921.

—— (1994). 'On Behalf of naïveté', in J. A. C. Baum and J. V. Singh (eds.), *Evolutionary Dynamics of Organizations*. London: Oxford University Press, pp. 205–20.

—— (1996). 'Unlearning Ineffective or Obsolete Technologies', *International Journal of Technology Management*, 11: 725–37.

—— (2000). 'Is Janus the God of Understanding?', in T. Lant and Z. Shapira (eds.), *Managerial and Organizational Cognition*. Hillsdale, NJ: Lawrence Erlbaum, pp. 351–65.

—— (2003*a*). 'The Origins of Organization Theory', in H. Tsoukas and C. Knudsen (eds.), *The Oxford Handbook of Organization Theory: Meta-theoretical Perspectives*. Oxford: Oxford University Press, pp. 143–82.

—— (2003*b*). 'Turning Lemons into Lemonade: Where is the Value in Peer Reviews?', *Journal of Management Inquiry*, 12: 344–51.

—— (2004). 'Why I Stopped Trying to Understand the Real World', *Organization Studies*, 25(7): 1233–54.

—— (2005). 'How Much Better are the Most Prestigious Journals? The Statistics of Academic Publication', *Organization Science*, 16: 180–200.

—— and Bass, F. M. (1967). 'An Experimental Study of Risk-Taking and the Value of Information in a New Product Context', *Journal of Business*, 40: 155–65.

—— and Dutton, J. M. (1971). 'The History of Simulation Models', in J. M. Dutton and W. H. Starbuck (eds.), *Computer Simulation of Human Behavior*. New York: Wiley, pp. 9–102.

—— and Hedberg, B. L. T. (2001). 'How Organizations Learn from Success and Failure', in M. Dierkes, A. Berthoin Antal, J. Child, and I. Nonaka (eds.), *Handbook of Organizational Learning and Knowledge*. Oxford: Oxford University Press, pp. 327–50.

—— and Mezias, J. M. (1996). 'Opening Pandora's Box: Studying the Accuracy of Managers' Perceptions', *Journal of Organizational Behavior*, 17(2): 99–117.

—— and Milliken F. J. (1988). 'Challenger: Changing the Odds Until Something Breaks', *Journal of Management Studies*, 25: 319–40.

—— Greve, A., and Hedberg, B. L. T. (1978). 'Responding to Crises', *Journal of Business Administration*, 9(2): 111–37.

Staw, B. M. (1976). 'Knee-Deep in the Big Muddy: A Study of Escalating Commitment to a Chosen Course of Action', *Organizational Behavior and Human Performance*, 16: 27–44.

—— McKechnie, P. I., and Puffer, S. M. (1983). 'The Justification of Organizational Performance', *Administrative Science Quarterly*, 28: 582–600.

Stogdill, R. M. (1948). 'Personal Factors Associated with Leadership: A Survey of the Literature', *Journal of Psychology*, 25: 35–71.

—— and Coons, A. E. (1957). *Leader Behavior*. Columbus, OH: Ohio State University, Bureau of Business Research.

Sullivan, J. W. N. (1928). *The Bases of Modern Science*. London: Benn.

Sutcliffe, K. (1994). 'What Executives Notice: Accurate Perceptions in Top Management Teams', *Academy of Management Journal*, 37: 1360–78.

Sutton, R. I. and Rafaeli, A. (1988). 'Untangling the Relationship Between Displayed Emotions and Organizational Sales: The Case of Convenience Stores', *Academy of Management Journal*, 31: 461–87.

Task Force on Statistical Significance, Board of Scientific Affairs (1996). *Initial Report*. Washington, DC: American Psychological Association, www.apa.org/science/tfsi.html.

Tatsuoka, M. M. (1993). 'Effect Size', in G. Keren and C. Lewis (eds.), *A Handbook for Data Analysis in the Behavioral Sciences, Vol. 1: Methodological Issues*. Hillsdale, NJ: Erlbaum Associates, pp. 461–79.

Thompson, B. (2002). 'What Future Quantitative Social Science Research could Look Like: Confidence Intervals for Effect Sizes', *Educational Researcher*, 31(3): 24–31.

Thorndike, E. L. (1911). *Animal Intelligence*. New York: Macmillan.

Thune, S. S. and House, R. J. (1970). 'Where Long-Range Planning Pays Off', *Business Horizons*, 13(4): 81–7.

Tolman, E. C. (1948). 'Cognitive Maps in Rats and Men', *Psychological Review*, 55: 189–208.

Tosi, H., Aldag, R., and Storey, R. (1973). 'On the Measurement of the Environment: An Assessment of the Lawrence and Lorsch Environmental Uncertainty Subscale', *Administrative Science Quarterly*, 18: 27–36.

Van Valen, L. (1973). 'A New Evolutionary Law', *Evolutionary Theory*, 1: 1–30.

Voltaire [F. M. Arouet] (1756). Chapter I, Part I of *Candide; or, the Optimist*.

Vroom, V. H. and Yetton, P. W. (1973). *Leadership and Decision-making*. Pittsburgh: University of Pittsburgh Press.

Walster, E., Berscheid, E., and Walster, G. W. (1973). 'New Directions in Equity Research', *Journal of Personality and Social Psychology*, 25: 151–76.

Watzlawick, P., Weakland, J. H., and Fisch, R. (1974). *Change: Principles of Problem Formation and Problem Resolution*. New York: Norton.

Weber, M. (1947). *The Theory of Social and Economic Organization*. London: Collier-Macmillan.

Webster, E. J. and Starbuck, W. H. (1988). 'Theory Building in Industrial and Organizational Psychology', in C. L. Cooper and I. Robertson (eds.), *International Review of Industrial and Organizational Psychology 1988*. London: Wiley, pp. 93–138.

Wesman, A. G. and Bennett, G. K. (1959). 'Multiple Regression vs. Simple Addition of Scores in Prediction of College Grades', *Educational and Psychological Measurement*, 19: 243–6.

Whitehurst, G. J. (1984). 'Interrater Agreement for Journal Manuscript Reviews', *American Psychologist*, 39: 22–8.

Whittington, C. J., Kendall, T., Fonagy, P., Cottrell, D., Cotgrove, A., and Boddington, E. (2004). 'Selective Serotonin Reuptake Inhibitors in Childhood Depression: Systematic Review of Published Versus Unpublished Data', *The Lancet*, 363(9418): 1341.

Whyte, W. H., Jr. (1956). *The Organization Man*. New York: Simon & Schuster.

Wiener, N. (1948). *Cybernetics, or, Control and Communication in the Animal and the Machine*. Wiley-MIT.

Wilkinson, L. and Task Force on Statistical Inference (1999). 'Statistical Methods in Psychology Journals: Guidelines and Explanations', *American Psychologist*, 54: 594–604.

Wilson, S. (1955). *The Man in the Grey Flannel Suit*. New York: Simon & Schuster.

Winkler, R. L. (1984). 'Combining Forecasts', in S. Makridakis, A. Andersen, R. Carbone, R. Fildes, M. Hibon, R. Lewandowski, J. Newton, E. Parzen, and R. L. Winkler (eds.), *The Forecasting Accuracy of Major Time Series Methods*. Chichester: Wiley, 289–95.

—— and Makridakis, S. (1983). 'The Combination of Forecasts', *Journal of the Royal Statistical Society, Series A*, 146: 150–7.

Wold, H. O. A. (1965). 'A Graphic Introduction to Stochastic Processes', in H.O.A. Wold (ed.), *Bibliography on Time Series and Stochastic Processes*. Edinburgh, UK: Oliver and Boyd, 7–76.

Wolff, W. M. (1970). 'A Study of Criteria for Journal Manuscripts', *American Psychologist*, 25: 636–9.

Zukav, G. (1979). *The Dancing Wu Li Masters: An Overview of the New Physics*. New York: Bantam.

Index